W9-BQY-554

FROM THE LIBRARY OF
Paul Tittle

THE SECRETS OF A LASTING MARRIAGE

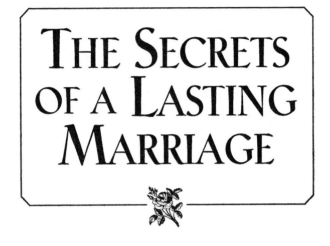

H. NORMAN WRIGHT

THE SECRETS OF A LASTING MARRIAGE

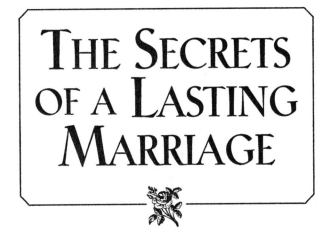

H. NORMAN WRIGHT

Regal Books
A Division of Gospel Light
Ventura, California, U.S.A.

Published by Regal Books
A Division of Gospel Light
Ventura, California, U.S.A.
Printed in U.S.A.

Regal Books is a ministry of Gospel Light, an evangelical Christian publisher dedicated to serving the local church. We believe God's vision for Gospel Light is to provide church leaders with biblical, user-friendly materials that will help them evangelize, disciple and minister to children, youth and families.

It is our prayer that this Regal book will help you discover biblical truth for your own life and help you meet the needs of others. May God richly bless you.

For a free catalog of resources from Regal Books/Gospel Light please contact your Christian supplier or call 1-800-4-GOSPEL.

The following Bible versions are used:
AMP. O.T.—From *The Amplified Bible, Old Testament.* Copyright © 1965, 1987 by The Zondervan Corporation. Used by permission.
AMP. N.T.—Scripture quotations are taken from the *Amplified New Testament,* copyright © 1954, 1958, 1987 by The Lockman Foundation. Used by permission.
KJV—King James Version. Authorized King James Version. Public Domain.
NASB—Scripture taken from the *New American Standard Bible,* © 1960, 1962, 1963, 1968, 1971, 1972, 1973, 1975, 1977 by The Lockman Foundation. Used by permission.
NIV—Scripture quotations are taken from the *Holy Bible, New International Version®. NIV®.* Copyright © 1973, 1978, 1984 by International Bible Society. Used by permission of Zondervan Publishing House. All rights reserved.
NKJV—From *The New King James Version.* Copyright © 1979, 1980, 1982, Thomas Nelson, Inc.
PHILLIPS—*The New Testament in Modern English,* Revised Edition, J.B. Phillips, Translator. © J.B. Phillips 1958, 1960, 1972. Used by permission of Macmillan Publishing Co., Inc., 866 Third Avenue, New York, NY 10022.
RSV—From the *Revised Standard Version* of the Bible, copyright 1946, 1952, and 1971 by the Division of Christian Education of National Council of the Churches of Christ in the USA. Used by permission.
TLB—Verses marked (*TLB*) are taken from *The Living Bible* © 1971. Used by permission of Tyndale House Publishers, Inc., Wheaton, IL 60189. All rights reserved.

© Copyright 1995 by H. Norman Wright
All rights reserved.

OVERTON MEMORIAL LIBRARY
HERITAGE CHRISTIAN UNIVERSITY
P.O. Box HCU
Florence, Alabama 35630

Library of Congress Cataloging-in-Publication Data
Wright, H. Norman.
    The secrets of a lasting marriage / H. Norman Wright.
        p. cm.
    ISBN 0-8307-1749-8 (hardcover)
    1. Marriage. 2. Marriage—Religious aspects—Christianity.
HQ734.W94917 1995   95-455
306.81—dc20   CIP

1 2 3 4 5 6 7 8 9 10 11 12 13 14 15 16 17 / 01 00 99 98 97 96 95

Rights for publishing this book in other languages are contracted by Gospel Literature International (GLINT). GLINT also provides technical help for the adaptation, translation and publishing of Bible study resources and books in scores of languages worldwide. For further information, contact GLINT, P.O. Box 4060, Ontario, CA 91761-1003, U.S.A., or the publisher.

CONTENTS

INTRODUCTION

An older couple you know, or see frequently as you go about your daily activities, has something very special to teach people today. I don't know their names or circumstance, and you may not either, but my experience in marriage counseling assures me they are there, in or near your life.

They may walk together, around the block or at the mall or the beach, arm in arm or holding hands. They may exchange knowing glances and half-smiles while in conversation with others. You may catch her smoothing an unruly wisp of his hair. He has an old-fashioned way of opening doors for her.

They so accurately anticipate what each other is saying or thinking that they often don't complete the sentences they start. A smile or a nod indicates the point is made. It's a kind of telepathy born of having spoken volumes to each other, and having learned each other's style of communication.

The couple I'm describing has been married thirty or forty or fifty years or even more.

They have a love that lasts.

Love that doesn't last gets so much more attention these days that you may think there are very few couples like this left. But the reason I'm confident you know one or more is that I've known them myself. And I think it's high time that a society in which half of the new marriages end in divorce get acquainted with this couple.

We need desperately to learn what kept them together through the years, some of which were very difficult. They stuck together through hard financial times, and wars, and sickness, and loss. Looking into their eyes you can sometime see remnants of pain, but somehow—unlike many modern marriages—it didn't create a wound between them that could not be healed.

In my work with couples, I believe I have found some characteristics of this couple's relationship that other marriages can use. So in this book we will be looking not at what makes marriages fail, but what makes them last. In the process I will challenge you, the reader, to call on every available resource, including the power of God and His Holy Spirit, to look at your own marriage in this positive light.

A great deal is at stake. You and your spouse can find greater joy by developing a love that lasts. As many current studies show, the children we used to say would "bounce back" from divorce, but who actually often suffer permanent damage, can be saved a great deal of pain when couples discover a love that lasts. Homes can be happier when they are characterized by long-term marriages. Opportunities for personal and interpersonal growth are so much greater in this kind of marriage.

As Christians, discovering a love that lasts is important for another reason that is often overlooked. We need to love forever because that's how God loves. *Whole marriages give glory to God, while broken marriages communicate the wrong message about Him.*

When the aged apostle John wrote to early Christians, he reflected profoundly on this topic of love. He said it is demonstrated in its highest degree by God's sending His own Son, Jesus, into the world. Then John states: "Love is made complete among us...*because in this world we are like him*" (1 John 4:17, *NIV*, italics added).

God started a vast circle of love in sending His Son. But as heavenly a concept as that is, think of this—John says that *this circle is completed by human love!* When two people give to each other in the way God gives to us, they demonstrate something of the love of God. And of course the reverse is true: When two believers fail to love, it's a bad reflection on the God who taught them to love.

Paul applied this principal to the Church when he urged Christians to "keep the unity of the Spirit through the bond of peace" (Eph. 4:3, *NIV*). Then follows that famous list of "ones"—one body, Spirit, hope, Lord, faith, baptism—and one *God and Father* (see vv. 4–6). Christian unity is based on the unity of God. Unlike pagan deities, God is One. And Christians who live as one body in the Church reflect that oneness. And when we are divisive, we still reflect a picture of the God we serve—although it is a very wrong picture. Divided, factious Christians give the impression they're getting their orders from differing gods!

In a similar way, Christian union in marriage is based on the unity of God. When a couple allows its immaturity or in-laws or selfishness or differing views of money management or child rearing or a host of other issues to drive it apart, it's not just a "this worldly" problem. The two are demonstrating that they may have a problem with God as well. Because despite the differences God has with us, He never gives up on His long-term love for us!

This book shows how you and your spouse can also develop a love that doesn't give up.

In chapter 1 we'll talk about the nature of that kind of love, and about the power of commitment. Chapter 2 helps you recall the love that brought you and your spouse together, and shows how to keep from falling out of love.

Getting down to practical, if not brass, tacks, chapter 3 answers the question of what makes a marriage work. Chapter 4 is designed to inspire in each of you a vision of what your marriage might be. And chapter 5 challenges you to probe your thought life to root out the kind of negative and false thinking that defeats so many marriages.

In chapter 6 we deal with the sticky wicket of change—transitions that can be either friends or foes. Working through individual differences is the focus of chapter 7, and rediscovering the positive steps that have previously worked in your marriage is the topic of chapter 8. Chapter 9 is about the all-important topic of the spiritual connection between you and your mate, and chapter 10 allows several of those couples I mentioned, whose love has lasted through the years, to tell you what worked for them.

So read on—if you care deeply not just about the first blush of love when it is beautiful and so very tender, but also about the maturing of a relationship into a love that lasts.

– 1 –

A LOVE THAT LASTS

The wonder and the promise of a love that lasts were once related to me in the writings of an older man. Listen to the message he gave to all of us as he wrote:

I couldn't even describe what I thought love was when I was first married. Forty years is a long time to be together with one person. It's almost half of a century. All I knew then was that I wanted a love that would keep us together forever. Jean really felt those love feelings a lot of people talk about. I'm not so sure I did. But I knew that I loved her. I just knew it. Jean described me as a "logical lover." I liked that. I still do. That's me all right. We learned it's all right to be different in the style of love we had and how we expressed it, as long as we were adaptable enough to learn to put it into a package that the other person liked. I didn't do that the first twenty years and that's what created what we now call our valley of "love recessions." Sometimes the wick of our candle of love got kind of low. But it never went out. We learned to work at our love and make it stronger. And it works, no matter what anyone says.

Now that we're almost in our seventies we don't know how many more years we'll have to love one another. But we'll make the most of them. I'm not a poet or much of a reader, never have been, but I found a statement that puts into words some of my thoughts better than I can. Maybe this will have a message to the next generation right behind us.

"It is love in old age, no longer blind, that is true love. For love's highest intensity doesn't necessarily mean it's highest quality. Glamour and jealousy are gone; and the ardent caress, no longer needed, is valueless compared to the reassuring touch

of a trembling hand. Passers-by commonly see little beauty in
the embrace of young lovers on a park bench, but the understanding smile of an old wife to her husband is one of the loveli-
est things in the world."
That sums it all up.[1]

A lasting love is possible, and it's also necessary. Commitment and love
go hand in hand. Just as commitment is a choice, so also is love. Love is not
just something that happens. It must be cultivated so it can grow.

ROMANCE VERSUS INFATUATION

As I work with young couples in premarital counseling, I push them to evaluate whether what they are calling love is really love. If it's infatuation, then
both it and the relationship will die. There is a blindness to infatuation that
makes people see what they want to see. Later they discover what they
thought they saw is not what they got. When their infatuation dies, it's like
stepping out of a plane without a parachute. The trip down is long and painful.

The longer we are married the more we understand (hopefully!) about the
kind of love that binds us together when we are at our best and at our worst.
As a personal friend put it, "There are many times when we look at each
other and there is no physical or passionate response. That's OK. It's been
there before and it will be there again. We're not threatened when it's not
because we know that we love each other. That's permanent, lasting. And we
think it's also a gift from God. And for that we rejoice."

When couples begin their lives together there is usually a sense of
romantic or passionate love. That's good. For many people that's how it
begins. It can be the overture that comes before the main event—lasting love.
Romance and passion are easy; love is work. The difference is, "Romance is
based on sexual attraction, the enjoyment of affection and imagination. Love
is based on decisions, promises, and commitments."[2]

There is a benefit to romantic or passionate love. Dr. Neil Warren suggests that:

> ...passionate love performs a powerful service as long as it lasts.
> It focuses the total attention of two people on each other long
> enough for them to build an enduring structure for their relation-
> ship. The passionate love experience will never hold the two of
> them together forever. But building "enduring structures" for a
> relationship takes a lot of time and effort, and if two people are not
> attracted to one another physically, the hard work might never get
> done. That's another function of passionate love—the life-chang-

ing experience of being accepted and valued. When two people find themselves totally engrossed in each other, they often experience a dramatic boost in their self-esteem. For in the process of discovering that someone else finds them attractive, they begin to see themselves as attractive, too. Passionate love focuses a bright, positive light on each of the persons involved, and both of them fall in love not only with each other, but also with themselves.[3]

It does help to have some natural physical attraction or emotional response.

THE FRIENDSHIP OF MARRIAGE

What kind of love helps a marriage last? You may be surprised, because I'm not going to begin with *agape*, which is what most people expect. I'm starting with another kind of love—friendship love. Why? Because in a national study of hundreds of couples who had fulfilling marriages, couples were given thirty-nine factors that would best explain the success of their marriages and why they were successful whereas others were not. Both husbands and wives were asked to put these factors in order of importance for their marriages. The fascinating fact was that the top seven selected by both husbands and wives were the same. But the first and second choices reflect the type of love we're considering here. They were "My spouse is my best friend" and "I like my spouse as a person."[4]

This love is *phileo* love. *Philos* is a biblical word for friendship love. Whereas romantic love cannot sustain a relationship, companionate or friendship love can. A friend is someone you like to be with. You enjoy his or her company; you like his or her personality; you can play and work together. You have shared interests. It's not that you are loved only because of what you share, but by sharing you develop a different kind of love. It means companionship, communication, and cooperation. One writer describes it as "companionate love."

> This may be defined as a strong bond, including a tender attachment, enjoyment of the other's company and friendship. It is not characterized by wild passion and constant excitement, although these feelings may be experienced from time to time. The main difference between passionate and companionate love is that the former thrives on deprivation, frustration, a high arousal level, and absence. The latter thrives on contact and requires time to develop and mature.[5]

I have seen numerous marriages over the years fall apart not only because this type of love was nonexistent, but because the couples weren't even sure how to develop it. When *phileo* or companionate love has developed, couples will have this to stabilize their relationships when the romantic love fades. Unfortunately, some with certain personality proclivities are almost addicted to the "high" or excitement of romantic love, and when it diminishes, they fall apart or bail out to seek new and exciting relationships.

Requirement: Friendship

What does friendship love entail? It's an unselfish dedication to your partner's happiness. It's when the fulfillment of his or her needs becomes one of your needs. It's learning to enjoy what he or she enjoys, not just to convince him or her that you're the right person, but to *develop* the enjoyment yourself as you share the enjoyment together.

I love trout fishing. Because of my wife's unselfish friendship-love, she developed a liking for trout fishing, too. Now she even has her own set of waders and a float tube. Recently she asked me to take her to Alaska for salmon fishing sometime!

I have genuinely learned to enjoy art and fine paintings from Joyce. We both learned, and it brought us closer together. Friendship means you do some things together, but you're also comfortable with having your own individual interests and you encourage each other in these. There is a balance between togetherness and separateness.

Requirement: Intimacy

Friendship-love involves a certain level of intimacy in which there is openness, vulnerability, and emotional connection. You also share goals, plans, and dreams, and work together.[6]

A marriage that lasts is a marriage that has a husband and wife who are friends. In fact, a marriage that begins with friendship as the initial relationship, with romance developing later, is the ideal basis for a marriage. As a friendship develops over the years, the real evidence is there when you choose each other for just the joy of the other person's company. Some couples have said they are friends, but sometimes I wonder if they would be if their sexual or household dependencies didn't exist.

Requirement: Practice

Friendship in marriage means that you practice it. Friendship is part of God's intention for marriage. There is a vow of trust. You don't become selfishly competitive, but wish your partner the best. You share each other's happiness and rejoice in it almost as much as the other does.

A friend doesn't automatically approve of everything we do or say, and that's all right. Friends don't attempt to control each other, because they respect each other too much. Friends try to understand the other's preferences. They can disagree and it doesn't damage the relationship. To be a friend you have to be able to take the other person's point of view. Becoming a friend necessitates changing old habits and beliefs.

Recently I read an interesting book on peer marriage. The word "peer" means one that is of equal standing with the other. The author felt there were several requirements to be fulfilled in order to have deep friendship in a marriage. Friendship in marriage means learning to express your romantic side in a way that meets your spouse's needs. It also means that both husband and wife are able to be a caregiver and a care receiver.

COUNTERFEIT LOVES

There are many expressions of love in marriage, some genuine and some counterfeit. Dr. Les Parrott effectively describes the counterfeit styles of love in his book *Love's Unseen Enemy* (Zondervan Publishers). Each style has several characteristics.

Pleasers

Unfortunately, some people equate marital love with being a pleaser. Pleasers are persons who are dominated and guided by their emotions. They do the right things for the wrong reasons. They do loving things rather than *being* loving persons.

Pleasers have this overwhelming need to please. It's as though they live to make people happy. As you watch them, they appear to be conscientious and caring. They go out of their way to make others—especially their partners—feel comfortable. They're especially good at remembering to do the little things others overlook. They're approachable and agreeable, and when asked to do something they usually do more than they're requested to do, and they do it with a warm smile.

But these acts of love aren't voluntary; they're compulsive. Such people feel personally responsible for the happiness of others. If their partners are unhappy, they feel guilty. They're driven to do too much so they will feel better. In a marriage they may end up feeling used. And...most pleasers tend to be women.

Pleasers are the givers of life. Hundreds of husbands and wives constantly give and give and give, but not because of love. It is either because of guilt or because they meet some of their own needs by giving. They need to give to others in order to feel good about themselves. It is like being hooked on helping. They become "helpaholics."

Pleasers try to avoid being receivers. When they must receive, they feel uneasy and guilty, and they begin thinking of ways to repay.

Pleasers have a performance mentality. They must do things right away, and they want to look good. They need approval from their partners in order to keep their guilt under control. They live for the applause. They also live with a fear of failure, and unfortunately this can drive them to comply with unrealistic requests for their help. Saying no to anyone is unheard of, because they view that as a personal failure. But this is not a healthy, biblical way to love another person.

Pleasers believe they're responsible for their spouses' well-being and happiness. It reminds me of a rescuer, a self-appointed lifeguard. But the ones they tend to rescue aren't drowning.

To pleasers, self-denial is not a means to an end, but an end in and of itself. But this makes loving behavior no longer loving. They turn into martyrs and, in the process, may drive others away. This in turn makes them feel more guilt so they try harder, which pushes others away even more. I've seen this happen again and again in marriages, and yet pleasers can't understand the negative effect of their behavior.

Pleasers are some of the great conflict avoiders of the world. They defer, give in, say yes when no is more appropriate, and allow wrong to continue. But they do have limits. If pushed or cornered into conflict, they either give in and blame themselves or erupt like a volcano because they're so unskilled in resolving conflicts.

In marriage, pleasers live for their partners' affections, holding on to any small measure they can get. But they also expect their partners to know what they want or need without ever telling them. Can you even imagine pleasers expressing what they need to their partners? Not really! Any withdrawal or diminishing of intimacy on the part of their partners is a disaster.

Time after time I have seen the same scenario played out in my office. The pleasing spouse sits there and says, "I just don't understand it. I love him so much, and I tried to please....Yet it seems that the more I try to please, the more I seem to push him away from me." It's true. The partner felt smothered and constricted.

One husband married to a pleaser told me, "It makes me sick. I wish she had more backbone and would stand up to me. Let's have some conflict. I'm tired of having a 'yes' person for a spouse." Pleasers tend to create some of the very problems they wish to avoid.

The Controller

Another counterfeit pattern is the *controller*. In many ways, this is the opposite of a pleaser. They both have a strong need for acceptance, but they certainly try to get it in different ways. Pleasers yield power to others in their desire to be loved, but controllers take over and take charge to gain the respect of others. A pleaser has an overabundance of sympathy but very little objectivity. The controller, being just the opposite, has a great amount of objectivity but doesn't know the first thing about sympathy. Controllers are very analytical. Even though this helps them understand the needs of others, the purpose is usually to gain control over them. Controllers can usually be identified by seven characteristics of how they relate to others.

1. *Their need to be in control is obvious.* They use two means to gain control. Fear expressed through intimidation is typical, and they are very adept at discovering and using weaknesses in other people. The other tool is to quietly silence their partners—by a word, a rolling of the eyes, or a gesture. Any mistake is noticed and used to guide the erring spouse into line with the controller's agenda.

2. *Controllers are very self-reliant.* For them, teamwork in a marriage is not possible. Totally independent, they create their own vacuums of loneliness, for their style of independence alienates them from others.

3. *Emotion is absent from their lives.* This helps to create marriages in which their partners end up starving for closeness and intimacy (see point 7). The emotional bonding that is necessary for a healthy relationship fails to happen. And all too often, controlling kills their spouses' love.

4. *They are inept at expressing loving behavior.* What may appear to be graciousness, politeness, kindness, or even being very sociable has a purpose in mind—to take control of the other person. Having love as an end result has no real meaning, but *using* love as a means to an end makes sense to them. If they show interest in another person, it's for a purpose. Their partners end up feeling used.

5. *Rules, rules, and more rules is their way of life.* And the more rigid they are the better. There is a right way to do things—it's their way, and it's the only way. They know what's best for others and will orchestrate their lives.

6. *Their style of communication is demanding in words, intent, and tone.* They're bottom-line people who cut right to the heart of a matter.

7. *Controllers won't open up and reveal their inner lives and feelings* for fear of losing their position of power or control. This makes it very difficult to develop intimacy in a marriage, especially when an overly dominant controller's partner is overly submissive. Even the submissive partner becomes fearful of being open and vulnerable, because he or she could be attacked and overwhelmed by the other person. There is a lack of mutuality in the marriage.

AGAPE LOVE IN MARRIAGE

Another form of love, agape, can increase our gratitude as well as our constant awareness and remembrance of God's agape love for us. An attitude of thankfulness for all of life develops. We're able to see and concentrate upon the positive qualities and attributes of our spouses, which we might overlook or take for granted. Our mind-sets and attributes can be refocused because of the presence of agape love. An attitude of appreciation causes us to respond with even more love toward our spouses.

Manifestations of Agape Love

Agape love manifests itself through several characteristics. First, it is an *unconditional* love. It is not based upon your spouse's performance, but upon your need to share this act of love with your spouse. If you don't, your spouse may live with the fear that you will limit your love if he or she does not meet your expectations.

Sometimes you have to learn to love your partner unconditionally. Here is what one husband said about how he learned to love in this way:

> When I married my wife, we both were insecure and she did everything she could to try to please me. I didn't realize how dominating and uncaring I was toward her. My actions in our early marriage caused her to withdraw even more. I wanted her to be self-assured, to hold her head high, and her shoulders back. I wanted her to be feminine and sensual.
>
> The more I wanted her to change, the more withdrawn and insecure she felt. I was causing her to be the opposite of what I wanted her to be. I began to realize the demands I was putting on her, not so much by words but by body language.
>
> By God's grace I learned that I must love the woman I married, not the woman of my fantasies. I made a commitment to love Susan for who she was—who God created her to be.
>
> The change came about in a very interesting way. During a trip to Atlanta I read an article in *Reader's Digest*. I made a copy of it and have kept it in my heart and mind ever since.
>
> It was the story of Johnny Lingo, a man who lived in the South Pacific. The islanders all spoke highly of this man, but when it came time for him to find a wife the people shook their heads in disbelief. In order to obtain a wife you paid for her by giving her father cows. Four to six cows was considered a high price. But the woman Johnny Lingo chose was plain, skinny, and walked with her shoulders hunched and her head down. She was very hesitant and shy. What surprised everyone was Johnny's offer—he gave eight cows for her! Everyone chuckled about it, since they believed his father-in-law put one over on him.
>
> Several months after the wedding, a visitor from the U.S. came to the islands to trade and heard the story about Johnny Lingo and his eight-cow wife. Upon meeting Johnny and his

wife the visitor was totally taken back, since this wasn't a shy, plain, and hesitant woman but one who was beautiful, poised, and confident. The visitor asked about the transformation, and Johnny Lingo's response was very simple. "I wanted an eight-cow woman, and when I paid that for her and treated her in that fashion, she began to believe that she was an eight-cow woman. She discovered she was worth more than any other woman in the islands. And what matters most is what a woman thinks about herself."

This simple story impacted my life. I immediately sent Susan flowers. (I had rarely if ever done that before.) The message on the card simply said "To My Eight-Cow Wife." The florist (who was a friend of mine) thought I had lost my mind and questioned if that was really what I wanted to say.

Susan received the flowers with total surprise and bewilderment at the card. When I returned from the trip I told her that I loved her for who she is and that I considered her to be my eight-cow wife, and then I gave her the article to read.

I now look for ways to show her that I am proud of her and how much I appreciate her. An example of this involved a ring. When we became engaged I had an antique engagement ring that I inherited from a great-great-aunt. Susan seemed very pleased and I never thought any more about it. But I had come out cheap, and that's how she felt. After twenty years of marriage, she shared with me how she felt about the hand-me-down wedding ring. We had our whole family get involved in learning about diamonds. Susan found what she liked. It was not the largest stone nor the most expensive. I would have gladly paid more. I bought it and gave it to her for Christmas. "To My Eight-Cow Wife, with all my love!" But what this did for our relationship is amazing.

First, it changed me! My desires began to change. My desire is now for Susan to be all that God has designed her to be. It is my responsibility as her husband to allow her that freedom.

It also changed her. Susan became free. She learned who she is in Christ. She has gained confidence and self-assurance. She is more aware of her appearance, her clothes, hair, makeup, because she is free to be who she is.

Susan rarely buys clothes for herself. Last year for Christmas I told her this year I would buy her an outfit or some type of clothing each month. This has boosted her confidence in her appearance. She looks great because she wants to!

Susan really is an Eight-Cow Wife of whom I am very proud. We have been married now since 1971.[7]

Agape love is given *in spite of how the other person behaves*. It is a gift, rather than something that is earned. You are not obligated to love. This form of real love is an unconditional commitment to an imperfect person. And it will require more of you than you ever realized. But that's what marriage is all about.

Agape love is also *a transparent love*. It is strong enough to allow your partner to get close to you and inside you. Transparency involves honesty, truth, and sharing positive and negative feelings. Paul Tournier shared the story of a woman whose mother gave her this advice: "Don't tell your husband everything: To maintain her prestige and keep her husband's love, a woman must retain a mystery for him." Tournier commented, "What a mistake! It fails to recognize the meaning of marriage and the meaning of love. Transparency is the law of marriage and the couple must strive for it untiringly at the cost of confessions which are always new and sometimes very hard."[8]

Agape love has *a deep reservoir to draw from*, so no matter what occurs, the love is felt and provides stability during times of stress and conflict.

Agape kindness is *servant power*. Kindness is love's willingness to enhance the life of another.

Chuck Swindoll describes this willingness:

> Anne Morrow was shy and delicate. Butterfly like. Not dull or stupid or incompetent, just a quiet specimen of timidity. Her dad was ambassador to Mexico when she met an adventurous young fellow who visited south of the border for the U.S. State Department. The man was flying from place to place promoting aviation. Everywhere he went he drew capacity crowds. You see, he had just won $40,000 for being the first to cross the Atlantic by air. The strong pilot and the shy princess fell deeply in love.
>
> When she became Mrs. Charles Lindberg, Anne could have easily been eclipsed by her husband's shadow. She wasn't, however. The love that bound the two together for the next forty-seven years was tough love, mature love, tested by triumph and tragedy alike. They would never know the quiet comfort of being an anonymous couple in a crowd. The Lindberg name didn't allow that luxury. Her man, no matter where he went, was news, forever in the limelight...clearly a national hero. But rather than becoming a resentful recluse or another nameless face in a crowd of admirers, Anne Morrow Lindberg

emerged to become one of America's most popular authors, a woman highly admired for her own accomplishments.

How? Let's let her give us the clue to the success of her career. "To be deeply in love, of course, is a great liberating force and the most common experience that frees....Ideally, both members of a couple in love free each other to new and different worlds. I was no exception to the general rule. The sheer fact of finding myself loved was unbelievable and changed my world, my feelings about life and myself. I was given confidence, strength, and almost a new character. The man I was to marry believed in me and what I could do, and consequently I found I could do more than I realized.

Charles did believe in Anne to an extraordinary degree. He saw beneath her shy surface. He realized that down in her innermost well was a wealth of wisdom, a deep, profound, untapped reservoir of ability. Within the security of his love she was freed—released—to discover and develop her own capacity, to get in touch with her own feelings, to cultivate her own skills, and to emerge from that cocoon of shyness a beautiful, ever-delicate butterfly whose presence would enhance many lives far beyond the perimeter of her husband's shadow. He encouraged her to do her own kind of flying and he admired her for it.

Does that imply she was a wild, determined, independent wife, bent on "doing her own thing," regardless? Am I leaving that impression? If so, I'm not communicating clearly. Such would be an inaccurate open portrait of Anne Morrow Lindberg. She was a butterfly, remember...not a hawk.

Make no mistake about it, this lady was inseparably linked in love to her man. In fact, it was within the comfort of his love that she gleaned the confidence to reach out, far beyond her limited, shy world.

We're talking roots and wings. A husband's love that is strong enough to reassure yet unthreatened enough to release. Tight enough to embrace yet loose enough to enjoy. Magnetic enough to hold, yet magnanimous enough to allow for flight...with an absence of jealousy as others applaud her accomplishments and admire her competence. Charles, the secure, put away the net so Anne, the shy, could flutter and fly.[9]

Agape love is the readiness to move close to another and allow him/her to move close to you. Agape is trying to be content with those things that don't live up to your expectations.

Agape love must be at the heart of a marriage. It's a self-giving love that keeps on going even when the other person is unlovable. This love will keep the other types of love alive. It involves kindness and being sympathetic, thoughtful and sensitive to the needs of your loved one, even when you feel he or she doesn't deserve it.

Think about this:

> Love means to commit yourself without guarantee, to give yourself completely in the hope that your love will produce love in the loved person. Love is an act of faith, and whoever is of little faith is also of little love. The perfect love would be one that gives all and expects nothing. It would, of course, be willing and delighted to take anything it was offered, the more the better. But it would ask for nothing. For if one expects nothing and asks nothing, she can never be deceived or disappointed. It is only when love demands that it brings on pain.[10]

Agape's Power

Since agape love is the heart of the marital love relationship, let's think some more about this wonderful gift.

Agape love is a healing force. To demonstrate the power of this love let's apply it to a critical area that affects marriage—irritability. Irritability is a barrier, and it keeps others at a distance if they know it is present within us. It is the launching pad for attack, lashing out, anger, sharp words, resentment, and refusal of others' offers to love us.

Agape love is unique in that it causes us to seek to meet the needs of our mate rather than demanding that our own needs be reciprocated. Our irritability and frustrations diminish because we are seeking to fulfill another rather than pursuing our own needs and demanding their satisfaction.

The Need to Express Agape

No matter how deep your love for your spouse may be, it will be unknown to him/her unless it is openly and consistently expressed in a manner that registers with your partner. Far too many marriage partners are silent and passive in their expressions of love. God has called us to be vessels of love pouring out generously to our partners. Marriage is God's creative gift to us, providing us the opportunity to express love to its fullest in the safety and security of an abiding relationship. And we are only able to love because He first loved us. His love is so extensive that it can heal the loveless experiences of the past. We no longer need to be dominated by hurtful memories. Instead, we can live and love knowing the adequacy of Jesus Christ in our lives.[11]

So liberating is this miracle of loving and being loved that it is something of which a husband and wife will take great joy in reminding one another. Indeed, one of the most important tasks for a couple to fulfill is this work of telling one another their love, which at heart is the wonderful reminder that they each are loved by God. This will not always be a pleasant or an easy task: Sometimes, to be sure, when a wife says, "I love you," it is something that a husband does not want to hear, at times something that he almost cannot bear to hear. He is tired of hearing it. He doesn't want to think about what it means. He does not want to let go of whatever it is that is preventing him from accepting it. He doesn't have the time or the energy to make a response. He doesn't want to be bothered with it. It is one more responsibility he can do without. He is not in the mood to be loved, let alone to love anyone else.

Still in spite of all resistance, the words of love are important. It is important that they be heard, and it is important that they be spoken, out loud, no matter how painful this hearing and this speaking might be. It is a marvelous thing when love comes bubbling up like tears in the throat as one is gripped by a sudden stabbing realization of the other's beauty and goodness, of how incredibly precious they are.[12]

Do you know how love is expressed? It is expressed through the ears. It is expressed with the eyes. When you give attention, you give affection. It is expressed in time scheduled and availability offered. It's the assurance that each will be there for the other.[13]

We have all been called to be people of love. Love is actually a commandment from God. Again and again in Scripture Jesus calls us to love:

Jesus replied: "'Love the Lord your God with all your heart and with all your soul and with all your mind.' This is the first and greatest commandment. And the second is like it: 'Love your neighbor as yourself.' All the Law and the Prophets hang on these two commandments" (Matt. 22:37-39, *NIV*).

Conclusions About Agape

Because love is a commandment, there are three conclusions that can be drawn from it.[14]

Loving others is a moral requirement. It is our responsibility to love even if others don't love us. This is an important principle when the love in your reservoir is low.

Love is an act of the will. We choose to love in our hearts and minds. You choose to think a certain way about your spouse. Love means choosing what is right and best to do rather than what you may want or feel like doing. It is this choice that will keep many marriages alive.[5]

Love is not determined by our feelings. Nowhere in Scripture does it say to love others if you feel like it. We can't command our feelings. They come and go. They're like the tide in the ocean; they come in and then recede. Don't allow your feelings to be your guide. I've had a number of spouses say, "My feelings of love for that person are gone." The shock on their faces is evident when I say "great." Now they can learn true love if they haven't already. And it does happen.

THE GLUE OF COMMITMENT

What I'm going to say now is going to sound contradictory, but here it is. The glue that will keep marriage together is *not* love.

There is a word that is becoming foreign in meaning and application to our culture in general—it's the word "commitment." Oh, I hear many who say they can commit to someone or something, and their commitment is in place when everything is going well. But it's when things get tough that the true level of commitment is evident.

Is Marriage a Contract?

Some psychologists, marriage counselors, and ministers have suggested that marriage is a contract, and many people are quick to agree. But is this really true? Is marriage really a contract?

In every contract there are certain conditional clauses. A contract between two parties, whether they be companies or individuals, involves the responsibility of both parties to carry out their parts of the bargain. These are conditional clauses or "if" clauses. If you do *this*, the other person must do *this*, and if the other person does *that*, you must do *that*. But in the marriage relationship there are no conditional clauses. Nowhere in the marriage ceremony does the pastor say, "If the husband loves his wife, then the wife continues in the contract." Or, "If the wife is submissive to her husband, then the husband carries out the contract."

In most contracts there are escape clauses. An escape clause says that if the party of the first part does not carry out his or her responsibilities, then the party of the second part is absolved. If one person does not live up to his or her part of the bargain, the second person can get out of the contract. This is an escape clause. In marriage there is no escape clause.

Marriage is not a contract. It is an unconditional commitment into which two people enter.

The Meaning of Commitment

Commitment means many things to different people. For some, the strength of their commitments varies with how they feel emotionally or physically. But the word "commit" is a verb and means "to do or to perform." It is not based primarily on feelings. It is a binding pledge or promise. It is a private pledge you also make public. It is a pledge carried out to completion, running over any roadblocks. It is a total giving of oneself to another person. Yes, it is risky, but it makes life fulfilling.

Commitment means giving up the childish dream of being unconditionally accepted by your partner who will fulfill all your needs and make up for all your childhood disappointments. It means expecting to be disappointed by the other, learning to accept this, and not using it as a reason to pull the plug.[6]

Perhaps a better way to describe this is to compare it to bungee jumping. If you've ever taken the plunge, you know that when you take that step off the platform you are committed to following through. There is no more time to think it over or change your mind. There is no turning back.

A friend of mine shared with me what has made his marriage last. He said, "Norm, we each had a commitment to each other and to the marriage. When our commitment to each other was low, it was the commitment to the marriage that kept us together."

Commitment to another person until he or she dies seems idealistic to some. When it suits us and we're not inconvenienced by it, we keep it. But when certain problems occur, it's not valid.

Commitment is more than continuing to stick it out and suffer with a poor choice of a spouse. It's not just maintaining; it's investing. It's not just enduring; it's working to make the relationship grow. It's not just accepting and tolerating negative and destructive patterns on the part of your spouse; it's working toward change. It's sticking to someone regardless of circumstances. A wife once shared this story with me in a letter:

> In 1988, I was diagnosed with Epstein Barr Virus (Chronic Fatigue Syndrome). It really changed my life, which had been filled with excitement and vibrancy. My husband, Kelly, has stood with me and become my protector through these past years of adjustment. He has taken care of our family when my strength would not allow me. He has held my hand through depression, including ten days in the hospital. He has insisted I get needed rest, even if it put more of a burden on him. He has paid the price of any hopeful cure we have found, no matter the cost. He has been more than a husband; he has been my best friend—a friend that has stayed closer than any family member.

He was my "knight in shining armor when I met him" and he has proven to be so throughout our fourteen-and-a-half years of marriage. I sometimes tell him that he has been "my salvation," because I don't know that I would still be going on if it weren't for his strength. I don't know that I would still walk with the Lord if it were not for his encouragement. Knowing him has been the greatest experience in my life.

Commitment Through Change

Keep in mind there will be ups and downs throughout the life of your marriage. There will be massive changes, some predictable and others intrusive. They hold the potential for growth, but are risky at the same time. Many marriages die because too many choose to ignore the inescapable fact that relationships and people change.

A wife shared the following with the congregation at her son's church:

> Since we have been married fifty years, you can just imagine how much change we have gone through: three wars, eleven Presidents, five recessions, going from the model A to the moon, from country road to the information superhighway. While these changes around us have been great, the personal changes that God has enacted within us through each other have been even greater. Although we often couldn't see how God was working in our lives at that time, we look back now and realize that our marriage has been a school of character development. God has used my husband in my life, and he's used me in his life to make us more like Christ. So what are the lessons that we've learned about how God uses marriage to change us? There are many. Through fifty years of marriage we've learned that differences develop us, that crises cultivate us, and that ministry melts us together.
>
> First, God has used our differences to help us grow. There have been many, many crises that God has used to develop us and to grow us. The first one was the big, big one—the crisis of being separated as soon as we got married. Ours was a wartime romance. We met at church, dated two months, got married after three weeks of engagement, and just after two months of marriage, we didn't see each other for the next two years, for Jimmy was shipped to the South Pacific during World War II. When he returned two years later, we were total strangers, but we were married to each other!

How would you have handled that situation?

How do you handle change? How do you handle the difficult, sudden, and painful changes? You've got to be willing to face the fact that change exists—you will change, your marriage will change, your partner will want you to change, and you will want him or her to change.[7]

Donald Harvey, author of *The Drifting Marriage*, says,

> Making a commitment to marriage as an institution is not meant to be a sentencing. Its intent is to offer security and stability. All couples have conflicts. Every marriage has to make adjustments. Feeling secure in a mate's commitment to the marriage allows the opportunity for dealing with conflicts and for needed adjustments to occur. This is what makes marriage resilient.
>
> A marriage can endure many affronts, whether from within or without, if the commitment to marriage as an institution is strong. It takes this kind of commitment for growth to occur.[8]

The Security of Commitment

I like what Neil Warren has said about one of the advantages that commitment provides for a relationship:

> Commitment significantly eases the fear of abandonment. It is this fear that is central to so many persons. It is often the most potent fear of all.
>
> When we were young and unable to take care of ourselves, we worried about becoming lost in a crowd, forgotten while waiting to be picked up at school, or left alone by dying parents. Fears like these persist throughout our lives. We shudder at the very thought of abandonment.
>
> That's why a spouse's promise to remain devoted means so much. Your partner will be loyal through every kind of circumstance. That frees you in a radical way. It allows you to be yourself at the deepest of levels, to risk and grow, to be absolutely authentic without any fear of being abandoned.[9]

I think the following comments by a wife illustrate lifelong expression of love and commitment. After many years together, one partner in every marriage could experience in one way or another what this person did.

> Real life death scenes aren't like the movies. My husband, too tall for a regulation bed, lay with his feet sticking out of the covers. I stood clinging to his toes as though that would save his life.

I clung so that if I failed to save him from falling off the cliff of the present, of the here and now, we'd go together. That's how it was in the netherworld of the intensive care unit....

It seemed that the entire world had turned into night. Cold and black. No place you'd volunteer to enter. Doctors tried to be kind. Their eyes said, "This is out of our hands. There's nothing more we can do."

A nurse with a soft Jamaican lilt placed a pink blanket over my shoulders. Someone whispered, "It's just a matter of minutes."

Just a matter of minutes to tell each other anything we had ever forgotten to say. Just a few minutes to take an accounting of our days together. Had we loved well enough?[20]

There will always be unasked and unanswered questions because of our imperfections. But love and commitment that are renewed and expressed lessen the need to ask. Perhaps one husband's description of commitment sums it up best of all:

Commitment is dangerous. It can be exploited. If my wife takes my commitment for granted, she may rest too easily on her laurels. Perhaps commitment should be not simply to each other as we are but to the highest potentialities we can achieve together. Commitment then would be to marriage not simply as a status but as a dynamic process. Let me commit myself to a lifelong adventure, the adventure of living with this woman. The route of this adventure has been only dimly charted by those who have gone before. Because I am unique and my partner is unique, our marriage will also be unique. We commit ourselves to undertaking this adventure together, and to following wherever it may lead. Part of the excitement of marriage is not knowing in advance what either the joys or the sorrows will be. We can be sure, however, that we will be confronted with countless challenges. Commitment provides the momentum for going forward in the face of those challenges.[21]

Well, that's a start on understanding what makes marriages last—love and commitment. Perhaps we should call these requirements the framework for a marriage. Now we need to consider the day-to-day elements that help to keep the framework in place. That's what our journey is all about for the remainder of this book.

NOTES

1. Original source unknown.
2. Thomas F. Jones, *Sex and Love When You're Single Again* (Nashville: Thomas Nelson Publishers, 1990), pp. 93–96.
3. From the book *Finding the Love of Your Life* by Dr. Neil Clark Warren and published by Focus on the Family. Copyright © 1992, Neil Clark Warren, pp. 81, 82. All rights reserved. International copyright secured. Used by permission.
4. Jeanette C. Laves and Robert H. Laves, *'Til Death Do Us Part* (Harrington, N.Y.: Park Press, 1986), p. 179, adapted.
5. Bernard I. Morstein, *Paths to Marriage* (Newbury Park, Calif.: Sage Publications, 1986), p. 110. Original source unknown.
6. Warren, *Finding the Love of Your Life*, pp. 97–99, adapted.
7. From *How to Change Your Spouse (Without Ruining Your Marriage)*, © 1994 by H. Norman Wright and Gary Oliver, Ph.D. Published by Servant Publications, Box 8617, Ann Arbor, Michigan 48107. Used with permission, pp. 24–25.
8. Paul Tournier. Original source unknown.
9. Taken from *Growing Strong in the Seasons of Life* by Charles R. Swindoll, Inc. Copyright © 1983 by Charles R. Swindoll, Inc. Used by permission of Zondervan Publishing House, pp. 66, 67.
10. David L. Leuche, *The Relationship Manual* (Columbia, Md.: The Relationship Institute, 1981), p. 3, adapted.
11. David Augsburger, *Sustaining Love* (Ventura, Calif.: Regal Books, 1988), p. 100, adapted.
12. Jones, *Sex and Love When You're Single Again*, pp. 86–87, adapted.
13. H. Norman Wright, *Finding Your Perfect Mate* (Eugene, Oreg.: Harvest House), 1955, material adapted.
14. H. Norman Wright, *Holding on to Romance* (Ventura, Calif.: Regal Books, 1992), p. 81. Used by permission.
15. Mike Mason, *The Mystery of Marriage: As Iron Sharpens Iron* (Portland, Oreg.: Multnomah Books, 1986), p. 65. Used by permission.
16. Rebecca Cutter, *When Opposites Attract* (New York: Dutton, 1994), p. 189, adapted.
17. Wright, *Finding Your Perfect Mate*, portions adapted.
18. Donald Harvey, *The Drifting Marriage* (Grand Rapids: Fleming H. Revell, 1988), p. 213.
19. Warren, *Finding the Love of Your Life*, p. 171.
20. Barbara Ascher, "Above All, Love," *Redbook* (February 1992).
21. *Marriage*, Second Edition by Robert O. Blood, Jr. Copyright © 1969 by The Free Press, a Division of Simon & Schuster, Inc., pp. 10–11. Reprinted with permission of the publisher.

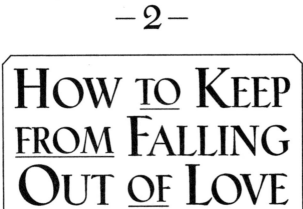

–2–

HOW TO KEEP FROM FALLING OUT OF LOVE

A wife shared with me, "I knew there would be disappointments and that John had flaws. During the first two years these became more evident, and each time they emerged I just took the attitude of 'I knew this beforehand. I'm just discovering them now. It's all right. I couldn't handle a perfect man anyway, because he's got to live with me. And I've got lots of flaws.' I guess that's what love is all about...loving a flawed person. I guess God knows all about that, too, doesn't He?"

Certainly He does. Yet God stays in love with us.

And for human beings to remain in love and have it continue to grow year after year, it is helpful to understand the steps involved in the death of love in a relationship. In fact, it isn't that difficult to predict which marriage relationships are most likely to have one person fall out of love with his or her partner. I have seen numerous people who have claimed to have "fallen out of love" with their spouses. This was usually something that had evolved over a period of years, until the person was apathetic and indifferent. One author describes "falling out of love" as marital dissatisfaction.[1]

Marital dissatisfaction can be described as the gradual loss of emotional attachment towards one's spouse. This encompasses diminished caring, emotional distancing, and over time, an increasing sense of apathy and indifference toward the other.[2] Those who are "socially committed" because of morality or the opinions of others choose to remain married, whereas others divorce quite readily. Often those who have less commitment to their partners as persons choose to exit from the relationships.

What happens to love in a marriage? There seems to be a process involved in the death of love that follows a pattern of five phases.

Phase I—Disillusionment

I think that almost everyone who marries eventually experiences some degree of disillusionment. The higher the level of expectations, the more idealistic the dreams, the less prepared a person is for the onset of this phase. When you don't expect or anticipate it, the devastation is worse.

Each phase carries with it the same pattern of *feelings, thoughts,* and ultimately, *behavior.* In this initial phase a person experiences disappointment that moves to disenchantment with marriage itself. During this time, spouses tend to compare their partners now with the way they were before they were married. Over the years I've heard many wives complain about the change they noticed in their husbands even during the first month. They said their husbands were open, feelings-oriented, communicative, and highly attentive during their courtship, but that within a month all that had disappeared.

Sometimes the partner has in fact changed, but sometimes it's only the perception spouses have of their partners' behavior. What they used to see as positive traits are now viewed as negative. As one husband said, "I knew she was organized and neat, but not to this extent. She's so rigid and perfectionistic, it's hard to live with her in the same house now."

When the feelings occur, *thoughts* that feed the disaffection process begin. At this phase, it's usually an increased awareness that the relationship isn't going as well as expected. This can lead to doubts about the persons they married as well as their decisions to marry them. Spouses use a number of coping strategies at this time. Some speak up, but many people tend not to say anything. Others use denial to cope. I've heard people make statements like the following:

"I told myself it just wasn't true. It was all in my head. It wasn't happening."

"I'm a peace-keeper anyway, so I didn't say anything. I just buried it. I thought it would get better. It didn't."

"For six years I kept all my feelings in. Then I discovered that just reinforced the problems."

The thoughts lead to various ways of *blaming.* Some try to change themselves. They feel some self-improvement would make a difference. They love more, try to be more attractive, or try to please even more than they have.

Some people tend to turn the responsibility outward and blame their partners, but many, especially women, blame themselves for the positions they're in. And when you take the responsibility for the problem you do the same for the solution. Unfortunately, women tend to do this more than men. This is consistent with our experience over the past thirty years that women are more likely than men to want to do something about marital problems. When husbands or wives attempt to "please" their partners in this way, they are conveying the message that when and if there are problems in the marriage, they'll take care of them. They assume the responsibility and this just perpetuates the problem.[3]

PHASE II—HURT

Hurt is the best way to describe the second phase of the death of love, which can overlap the first phase. The feelings in this phase include loneliness, being treated unfairly and unjustly, and a sense of loss. Often the person doesn't identify this as a loss or perceive what the loss involves. Now the thoughts expand to include more negatives such as the following:

"My spouse just doesn't understand me. That's unfair. He/she should understand."

"My needs are not being met by my spouse and they should be."

"I must not be very important to my spouse or he/she would be acting differently."

Frequently persons suffering in this phase begin to think about what the relationship is costing them and what they are getting out of it. Usually they feel they have ended up with the short end of the stick.

This is where the "old nature" of man begins to kick in. We all have a bent or inclination toward negative thinking. It's one of the effects of the fall of man. You begin to use a wonderful gift that God has given you—the imagination—in a negative manner. We all talk to ourselves. That's a given. But too often, unfortunately, the content is negative.

Man has struggled with this since Genesis 6:5: "The Lord saw that the wickedness of man was great in the earth, and that every imagination and intention of all human thinking was only evil continually" (*AMP*). Scripture again and again points out the importance of our thoughts and how they need to be controlled. "As he thinketh in his heart, so is he" (Prov. 23:7, *KJV*). We also find that "The thoughts of the righteous are right: but the counsels of the wicked are deceit" (12:5, *KJV*). "Search me, O God, and know my heart! Try me and know my thoughts!" (Ps. 139:23, *RSV*). "Gird your minds for action" (1 Pet. 1:13, *NASB*). *Gird* means mental exertion or putting out of the mind anything that could be hindering the Christian life.

There's a strong interrelationship between thoughts, feelings, and behaviors. Most of our emotions or feeling responses come from our thought lives; what we dwell upon, that we think about, can stimulate feelings. The words *think, thought,* and *mind* are used more than 300 times in Scripture. Often, a person's thoughts generate both feelings and behaviors, then the behavior becomes a reinforcer of the feelings and thoughts. And then the cycle repeats: The feeling intensifies or reinforces a particular thinking pattern and thus the behavior. Perhaps we see this pattern more in the marital relationship than elsewhere. Chuck Swindoll put it so well, as he usually does:

Thoughts, positive or negative, grow stronger when fertilized with constant repetition. That may explain why so many who are gloomy and gray stay in that mood, and why others who are cheery and enthusiastic continue to be so, even in the midst of difficult circumstances. Please do not misunderstand. Happiness (like winning) is a matter of right thinking, not intelligence, age, or position. Our performance is directly related to the thoughts we deposit in our memory bank. We can only draw on what we deposit.

What kind of performance would your car deliver if every morning before you left for work you scooped up a handful of dirt and put it in your crankcase? The fine-tuned engine would soon be coughing and sputtering. Ultimately, it would refuse to start. The same is true of your life. Thoughts about yourself and attitudes toward others that are narrow, destructive, and abrasive produce wear and tear on your mental motor. They send you off the road while others drive past.[4]

To counter negative thoughts about our spouses, it would be helpful to consider once again words of Scripture, such as the following:

"Do not be conformed to this world but be transformed by the renewal of your mind" (Rom. 12:2, *RSV*).

"Set your minds on things that are above, not on things that are on earth" (Col. 3:2, *RSV*).

We all need a transformation of the mind to have the mind of Christ. Dr. Lloyd Ogilvie, former pastor of the First Presbyterian Church of Hollywood—and as of March 1995, chaplain of the United States Senate—said, "Each of us needs to surrender the kingdom of our mind to God." Right on.

In this hurt phase there are certain behaviors that tend to occur. To solve hurt feelings, another person (a confidant) is sought out in order to gripe and complain about how dissatisfying the marriage or spouse is. Attempts are made to change the relationship and make it better, as well as attempts to change one's partner. Personally I believe we can and need to help one another change (this is addressed elsewhere in this book). But when you approach it from a position of hurt, you usually use an approach that either reinforces the basic problem or makes it worse.

PHASE III—ANGER

The third phase is *anger*. It too can overlap with the previous phase as a husband or wife travels the road to the loss of love. The disillusionment diminishes and the hurt turns into anger. Hurt and anger frequently go hand in hand.

But anger doesn't have to kill a marriage. It can actually show that we still care about our partner and the relationship. It can be a sign that we're alive and well and want to have something better in the relationship. Anger causes us to assert ourselves in situations where we should. And if it's presented correctly it can actually be an invitation to negotiate.

This is the time when the phrase "I think I'm falling out of love" begins to emerge. As the disappointment and hurts continue, they tend to obscure the love that was there when the relationship began.

The feelings of this stage can best be described as resentment, indignation, or bitterness. And these feelings can deaden feelings of love. Why is it that Scripture tells us to never let these gain a foothold in our lives regardless of what the other person has done?

An abundance of thoughts reinforce the cycle. Trust is just about gone. A spouse is now looking at the accumulation of hurts, and feeling their combined impact. The focus is on what the partner has done or hasn't done, and blame is a consistent thought. As the spouse thinks about the other, negative thoughts outweigh the positive.

"He doesn't love me. He wants a maid and sex partner, not a wife."

"Why did I ever think she would love me? She doesn't ever say it or show it. Sometimes I could just throttle her. She's bankrupting me as well."

"Sometimes I wish he'd have an accident driving home. He deserves it."

"I didn't marry her for her to have an affair every six months. She thinks I don't know, but I do. How can she be loving to others when she's an iceberg to me?"

With feelings and thoughts like this, you can imagine what behaviors might happen at this time. By now the feelings are usually being expressed to the errant spouse—not in a way that draws the two closer, but in a way that tends to alienate them. Expressions of hurt, anger, and disappointment are usually presented in a critical way, and mingled with an air of disgust. It's not uncommon to avoid the partner; sexual involvement is either cut off or becomes a mechanical duty. There is a physical and emotional withdrawal from both the partner and the marriage. As one wife said, "How is it possible to physically respond to someone you've started to loathe? I can't even sleep in the same bed with him because I'm so angry at him."

This is a dangerous time in a person's life, for hurt and anger makes us vulnerable to seeking need fulfillment elsewhere. In the death of love, emotional desperation is usually present, and this is a major cause for affairs. This lack of need fulfillment and intimacy creates an intense vacuum. It contributes to alienation as well as resentment. One writer describes the process in this way:

> Affairs begin not just for sexual reasons but to satisfy the basic need we all have for closeness, goodness, kindness, togetherness—what I call the "ness" needs. When these "ness" needs

are not met on a regular basis in a marriage, the motivation may
be to find a person who will be good to us, touch us, hold us,
give us a feeling of closeness. Sexual fulfillment may indeed
become an important part of an extramarital relationship, but the
"ness" needs are, for most men and women I know, initially
more important.[5]

When resentment exists, there is a feeling of ill will toward the other, a
desire to make the spouse pay, and a rationalization or justification of what is
being done. "If my partner isn't fulfilling my needs or making me happy, I will
find satisfaction elsewhere. He (or she) is to blame for this." I've heard this
excuse time and time again. But there are other and better options. I've seen
many marriages even at this stage turn around and become what each partner
wanted to begin with.

Sometimes our anger isn't because of what our spouse has done or didn't
do. It's because of our own expectations. Often these are intermingled with
what is known today as *entitlement*. This says that the degree of your need or
desire justifies your demand that your partner supply that need. It's like saying, "I want it so bad that I'm entitled to have it." It confuses personal desire
with obligation on your partner's part. It's almost saying that our partners
have no right to say no. Have you ever thought about this? Our expectations
breed entitlement. Have you ever considered what your expectations are for
your partner? Are they reasonable and are they attainable? Anger can be
reduced when both expectations and our thoughts are rearranged. Consider
this everyday household situation that could lead to a deadening of feelings
between partners. This came from my client Joan's own words:

> Let me give you an example of what's been going on for months
> in one way or another. The other day I spent several hours
> cleaning the house. I slaved over each room until they were
> spotless. All I wanted was for Dave to notice. Later on I realized
> not only was I expecting it, I deserved it. And when all he did
> when he came home was mess up two rooms, flop in front of the
> TV and ask, "Where's dinner? I'm hungry," I blew! I was
> ticked. Later on I wrote in my journal and not only did I figure
> out what went wrong, I got some insight into what I could do
> differently the next time. I wrote down what my thoughts were.
> "He should have noticed all the work I did today. He should have
> thanked me for what I did. I deserved it. He shouldn't have been
> so insensitive and inconsiderate. He's so sloppy. And he'll
> probably want sex tonight. He can just wait." As I wrote, I didn't
> like what I had thought, but there it was.

Then when I wrote what I could do differently, I really liked what I created. And again it started with my thought life. Some of them were as follows: "I wish he would notice all my work. I wonder why it's so important for him to notice and then praise me. Am I doing this for him or for me? Perhaps I could find a different way to get him to notice what I do around the house. Perhaps I could bring in our camera or video and ask him if he would like to take a picture of a fantastically clean house and the housekeeper who created this wonder!" I also wrote out a statement that I am going to read several times on those days that I clean. It goes like this: "I want Dave to notice what I've done today. If he doesn't, that's all right. I can handle that, too. My happiness and sense of satisfaction doesn't depend on his response. I didn't clean it just for him. I did it because it needed to be done. I feel good about what I've done and the results. If he notices, that's just icing on the cake. I don't have to be upset over it."

This worked for Joan. Eventually Dave did notice, because she gave him a note that simply said, "I feel even closer to you than usual whenever you notice what I've done around the house." Change does happen.

PHASE IV—AMBIVALENCE

The fourth phase of love's loss is *ambivalence*. The feelings reflect a sense of turmoil, because they shift back and forth between despair and hope for both the marriage and the partner. We're indecisive and unsure about what to do. This state is also reflected in our thoughts as well. We wonder, *What will it take for this marriage to work?* and *Would it be best to just get out of this? I don't see it going anywhere.* We consider other options to staying with this person, but we are also aware of and think about how the divorce would affect us and others.

All these feelings and thoughts lead to a set of behaviors that could include counseling over what to do. Sometimes friends and relatives are made aware of what is occurring, and there may be consideration of another who might be a better choice for a spouse than the current partner. Once again, remember that these phases can overlap and it can all add up to a state of confusion.

PHASE V—THE DEATH OF LOVE

The final phase is what all this has been leading up to: disaffection or "the death of love." The only feelings left are those that reflect the death of what each hoped would be a happy and fulfilling relationship. Indifference, detachment, and apathy exist and that's about it. I've heard this expressed in many ways.

"I've had it. I have no more energy. Nothing I did worked and now it's over."

"I have nothing left to feel with. I'm numb. I never thought it would end up like this. But ten years is enough time to invest in a bankrupt situation."

"I can't even get angry at her anymore. There's nothing left and I'm moving on."

"I don't care what she says she'll do now. It's too late. I don't even want to try anymore. I've been rejected way too much."

The *thoughts* are reflective of the feelings. There is very little desire to be or try to be at all close to the spouse. In terms of our partners ever meeting our needs, it's a closed book as far as we're concerned. Nothing our spouses do will work, and besides, it's too late. We behave basically in an avoidance pattern. There's no interest in any physical contact. The couple lives under the same roof, but they live separate lives for the most part. They're married singles and any counseling undertaken at this point is for the purpose of getting out of the relationship.[6]

It may help to see this pattern in chart form.

WHAT KILLS LOVE IN A MARRIAGE: FIVE PHASES

I. Disillusionment
  A. Feelings—Disappointment
  B. Thoughts—Doubts or denial
  C. Behavior—Blame
II. Hurt
  A. Feelings—Loneliness, sense of loss, "it's unfair"
  B. Thoughts—"My needs aren't met, my spouse doesn't understand me, I must not be important"
  C. Behavior—Complain to others, try to change spouse
III. Anger (accompanied by "I think I'm falling out of love")
  A. Feelings—Resentment, indignation, bitterness (a "bitter" bank develops)
  B. Thoughts—Focused on what spouse has or hasn't done—constant blame
  C. Behavior—Expresses feelings; critical, physical and emotional withdrawal; vulnerable time; affair prone
IV. Ambivalence
  A. Feelings—Sense of turmoil, unsure, indecisive about what to do
  B. Thoughts—Wonder what to do. "What about divorce?"

C. Behavior—May seek counseling, tells friends and relatives
V. The Death of Love
A. Feelings—Indifference, detachment, apathy
B. Thoughts—Indifference, detachment, apathy. "Nothing will help."
C. Behavior—Separate lives or divorce

WHY LOVE DIES

Fortunately, not all couples experience this pattern. Why do some love relationships die and others live on? Are there any patterns or predictors that can be used to help avoid those behaviors that are so destructive? I hear this question frequently from young couples. It's a good question and there is good news. There are answers that can be used to prevent this from happening as well as to reverse the process. God does have a future for all marriages, but it must be a cooperative effort between the three of you: God, husband, and wife.

This entire book is actually about keeping love alive. So let's consider some specifics that are based both on my research and my own counseling experience.

Control Tactics
One of the main contributing factors to the death of love is a lack of mutuality in the marriage. This can involve a variety of behaviors, including overt acts of controlling one's spouse through disregard of his or her unique personality qualities, opinions, faith, desires, activities, or lifestyle. It can involve forcing one's partner to do something against his or her will. It may include criticism, blame, and put-downs. These are all control tactics. Control comes in many forms and disguises. Perfectionists have a tendency to want to control others.

A wife married for ten years described her life:

> Carl is just so critical and particular but not in a loud or angry way. He never raises his voice. But he looks at me, shakes his head, or rolls his eyes to show his disgust over what I've done. If not that, I get what I call the "soft lecture." He doesn't raise his voice, get angry, or sound firm. Rather, he talks in a soft, patient condescending tone of voice implying, "How could you have been so stupid?" Sometimes I get the silent treatment and some sighs. That's the signal for me to figure out what I've done wrong.
>
> There have even been times, believe it or not, when he has taken the fork out of my mouth because I'm eating too much, turned off the TV because I shouldn't be watching that program, or corrected my volume of talking in public. I'm tired of it. I'm tired of going along with what he's doing. I can't deny who I am and I can't live trying to figure out how to please him. Besides, I've

heard this so much I've begun to doubt myself. I've even thought, Maybe he's right. Maybe I need to do what he says. Maybe I am creating the problems. But fortunately I came to my senses.[7]

Some couples have observed that the control tactics of their partners became the deciding factor in the demise of their relationships. If you happen to be married to a controller or a perfectionist, see chapter 11 of the book *How to Change Your Spouse (Without Ruining Your Marriage)* (Servant Publications, 1994).

The Lack of Empathy
When one is a controller, one of the key ingredients of mutuality in marriage will be missing—empathy. Regard for others and the ability to enter into their feeling worlds are parts of empathy. With empathy you show you are interested in your partner's world as well as your own. Empathy means entering the private world of your partner and becoming comfortable with it. It also means moving into that world for a time without making judgments.

Empathy conveys an exceptionally important message to another person. It says, "You count. You're important and significant." It both validates and encourages the development of the partner's self-esteem. But controllers don't usually care about their partners' feelings.

The Lack of Intimacy
In any marriage in which one partner is dominant and the other is passive or submissive, one of the necessary foundations for the survival of the marriage is lacking—emotional intimacy. (The word "submissive" in this context is not the healthy, biblical definition, but refers to submission based on fear, inadequacy, and insecurity. It's the "keeping peace at any cost" response.)

Dominant persons are not about to open their lives and become vulnerable, because it would lessen their sense of power or control. And submissive partners learn not to reveal much, because it will probably be used against them in some way. Not only does the controlling partner restrict you from expressing who you are, you don't want to express yourself because of the repercussions.

POWER AND INTIMACY
(*Power*—the capacity to influence another.)

Style of Marriage	POWER	INTIMACY	Level of Intimacy
More or less equal			Deep levels can develop.
Dominant–submissive			Intimacy is avoided.
Warfare			Intimacy is impossible.
Fused			Intimacy is shaky and conditional.

The *more or less equal* style of a marriage relationship indicates a balanced power distribution. It is a complementary relationship. Both partners think of themselves as competent, and each sees the other person as competent, too. Each person has specific areas of expertise in which his or her views have greater weight than the other, but this is not threatening.

Some relationships are *explosive*. Both husband and wife have the freedom to initiate action, give advice, criticize, etc., but most of their behaviors are competitive. If one states that he has achieved a goal or progressed in some way, the spouse lets it be known that she, too, has attained similar success. Both make it a point to let the other know of his or her equal status.

When conflicts in such a relationship become fairly open and consistent, the relationship is in a *warfare* state. The couple does not have balance for the relationship because both are vying for the dominant position and exchanging the same type of behavior.

Finally, there is the *fused* relationship, in which each person shares some power. But in order to have power, they each give up some of their individual identity. Separateness does not exist because it seems dangerous, and consequently there is an unhealthy type of closeness. Sometimes individuals like this will say, "We are so close that we think alike, we feel alike, and we are completely one."[8]

And this contributes to another major reason for the death of love in a marriage—the lack of emotional intimacy. As we work with couples in premarital counseling, through the various tests and evaluation tools that are used, we can now predict the probability of this problem occurring in advance, and take corrective steps. Sometimes this happens because people have shut down emotionally due to the pain of childhood abuse. In other cases, especially with men, the development of the emotional side of their lives is basically stunted. They haven't been encouraged to develop it.

The lack of intimacy can mean the absence of emotional connectedness, no emotional support, the absence of significant communication, no romance, etc. When couples marry, one of their desires and one of the characteristics of such a relationship is the opportunity to fling open all the doors and share their innermost feelings. And this should be present. It's one of the reasons people marry, as well as an ingredient that keeps a couple together. Over the past twenty-five years of conducting marriage seminars across the country, I have found that the number one frustration wives reflect about their marriages is this lack of emotional intimacy. Usually it is because their husbands do not show their feelings.

"Nothing Happens"

One of the constant problems that I've heard from couples year after year is, "We never resolve our problems. It's not that we don't talk about them, it's just that nothing happens. They just go on and on." When this happens it's usually because of not understanding and accepting individual differences that then are reflected in a communication process that goes nowhere and accomplishes little. Constant unproductive attempts as well as the avoidance of conflict will soon move to emotional distancing and, ultimately, disaffection.

These are some of the major reasons for the death of love. Perhaps you've identified with some, but hopefully what has been described in this chapter has not been totally characteristic of your experience. If it is, your question is more than likely, "What can I do about it?"

WHAT CAN BE DONE?

Some couples seek out counseling because an objective person can be helpful. But often couples are able to bring about needed changes by their own efforts. How can one person make it happen? The following suggestions have been used by many to build their marriages.

The initial step is to *assume that both your partner and the marital relationship can change.* This may mean going counter to your thoughts as well as your feelings. If you're at the place of saying "It just isn't possible," assume that a miracle is going to occur in the future and begin living your life as though you expect it to happen. What I am suggesting is probably something that you haven't tried fully yet—but what you have been doing hasn't worked, has it? So you don't have that much to lose, do you?

The second step is to *have in your mind a small but reasonable change you would like to see happen in your relationship.* Keep in mind that for the marital relationship to change, it will be necessary for both you and your partner to change. And contrary to a popular damaging myth, it *is* possible to change your spouse. (Hopefully it will be for the best, but all too often it's negative.)

It is also biblically sound to work for change in your partner. Scripture says that we are to urge, encourage, entreat, advise, teach, admonish, and exhort one another (see Acts 18:27; Phil. 4:2; Col. 3:16; 1 Thess. 4:10; 5:11). Sometimes another person doesn't even realize that the change you are requesting is to his or her advantage. There are definite, specific, and positive ways for you to assist your partner in change. (Again, see *How to Change Your Spouse [Without Ruining Your Marriage].*)

Another step closely aligned to the previous one is to *change your perception of your partner.* Eliminate negative, degrading perceptions you have about your spouse. Focus on the qualities, strengths, and potential you believed were there years ago. You may find your highly developed negative thoughts intruding, but they can be eliminated.

Then *identify the extent of your anger and resentment pool.* To restore love, resentment and bitterness must be addressed and released. The longer you hold on to them, the more work will be involved in letting them go. One author suggests that those experiencing the death of love for their partners usually have a "bitter bank."⁹ This is an accumulation of the bitterness that has been collected over the years. But most are not that aware of it, because they have concentrated so much energy on blaming their partners. Their emotions are dominated by this bitterness. And all the time and energy that have gone into the bitterness keeps them from taking constructive, positive steps.

Often at this stage people have given up hope that their partners will ever change, and the next best thing, in their opinion, is to fantasize about life without their partners. They think about how much better life would be without their partners, and many (especially Christians) fantasize about them dying, because that's easier and more acceptable than divorce. The time and energy used in this way keep them from making positive changes in their lives and reinforces their feelings about the futility of the relationships. This is what bitterness can do.¹⁰ Bitterness and resentment need release. For most people, writing their anger in journals or nonmailed letters to their partners and then reading the words aloud in a room by themselves is a healthy step.

One final step is a very necessary part of releasing resentment. Not only is it important to express and give up feelings of resentment, it is also essential that you *project a positive response to your spouse*. Emptying the container of resentment is only half the battle. You need to fill that void with feelings and expressions of love, acceptance, forgiveness, and friendship.

A number of my clients have stated that they have neither positive nor negative feelings toward some individuals. They're blasé. But what they have really developed is a state of emotional insulation. Neutrality must be replaced by positive, productive feelings.

WRITING AWAY YOUR RESENTMENT

I often recommend an exercise that develops a positive response to a resented spouse as a means of finding and eliminating the last vestiges of resentment. Take a blank sheet of paper and write your spouse's full name at the top. Below the name write a salutation, as in a letter: Dear _____.

Under the salutation, write on the left side of the page, "I forgive you for..." Then complete the sentence by writing down everything that has bothered you over the years. For example, "I forgive you for always trying to control my life."

Next, stop to capture the immediate thought that comes to mind after writing the statement of forgiveness. Does the thought contradict the concept of forgiveness you have just expressed? Do you feel an inner rebuttal or protest of some kind? Is there any anger, doubt, or caustic feeling that runs against your desire to forgive? Write all these contradictory thoughts under-neath the "I forgive you for..." statement. Don't be surprised if your thoughts are so firm or vehement that it seems that you have not done any forgiving at all. Continue the exercise by writing the "I forgive you for..." statement, fol-lowed by your immediate thoughts, even if they are contradictory.

Keep repeating the process until you have drained all the pockets of resentment. You will know you have reached that point when you can think of no more contradictions or resentful responses to the statement of forgiveness you have written. Some people finish this exercise with only a few contradic-tory responses. Others have a great deal of resentment and use several pages to record their feelings.

The following is a typical example of how a husband forgave his wife for her coldness and critical attitude toward him, and for her extramarital affair. Notice how his protests and contradictions to forgiveness become progres-sively less intense. Finally his resentment drains away to the place where he can simply say "I forgive you" and feel no further need for rebuttal.

> Dear Liz, I forgive you for... *I'm hurt and angry. I've*
> *put up with you for years.*
> Dear Liz, I forgive you for... *How do I know I can trust*
> *you after what you did?*
> Dear Liz, I forgive you for... *How do I know you're going to*
> *be any different? I can't take*
> *your coldness anymore.*
> Dear Liz, I forgive you for... *I'm really hesitant to open*
> *myself up to you anymore.*
> *I want to love you, but*
> *I've been rejected so much.*
> *I'm afraid of being*
> *rejected again.*
> Dear Liz, I forgive you for... *I would like to forgive you at*
> *times. I don't like these*
> *feelings I have. It's a bit*
> *better as I write this. I feel*
> *a bit funny and awkward*
> *as I do this.*
> Dear Liz, I forgive you for... *I wish this had never*
> *happened.*
> Dear Liz, I forgive you for... *I know I've blamed you and I*
> *feel you're responsible. But*
> *maybe I contributed to the*
> *problems in some way.*

Dear Liz, I forgive you for... *My anger is less, and maybe
some day it will go away.*
Dear Liz, I forgive you for...
Dear Liz, I forgive you for...

Jim wrote this letter to Liz one day, then three days later he repeated the exercise. In his second letter, after writing eight contradictory thoughts, Jim was able to conclude with several "I forgive you..." statements with no rebuttals.

After completing your own version of this exercise, spend time in prayer asking God to help you completely release your anger and change your heart toward your partner. Then try to visualize your partner sitting in an empty chair, verbally accepting your forgiveness. Take as long as you need for this step, because it is very important. When you have finished the exercise, destroy your list of statements, without showing it to anyone, as a symbol that "old things are passed away; behold, all things are become new" (2 Cor. 5:17, *KJV*).

FEELING AND BEHAVING

Perhaps you're at a place where the hurt has been so painful that you're reluctant to try to rebuild your love. As one wife said, "Why should I reach out to him again? If I do and he doesn't respond, I'll just be hurt all over again. Sometimes enough is enough." If this is how you feel, admit it and accept your feelings. But stay away from the danger of believing that before you try again you need to wait until your feelings change. It just doesn't work that way. Nor does Scripture teach this.

If we behave in a loving manner it is more than likely that our feelings will begin to change. The principle is quite simple and all it takes is a decision on your part to do it. Invite the Holy Spirit to empower you. When you behave toward your spouse as if your loving feelings were alive and well (which can stimulate your partner's feelings), then the possibility of reviving your love for your spouse is possible.

The next step may create some tension within you, but it is a necessary step. It's called forgiveness. Forgiveness is many things. It is no longer being chained to the hurt you've experienced with your spouse. It is no longer using the wonderful gift of memory as a weapon. It is no longer hurting others as we have been hurt. It is making yourself vulnerable and open to being hurt again. It is as Lewis Smedes said:

...a new vision and a new feeling that is given to the person who
forgives....True forgivers do not pretend they don't suffer. They
don't pretend the wrong does not matter much....You will know

that forgiveness has begun when you recall those who hurt you and feel the power to wish them well."

Applying the various principles found throughout this book will help you in this process of restoring your love. (If your spouse is the one who has lost his or her love for you, the best resource for you to read is *Rekindled* by Pat Williams [Revell, 1985].)

In keeping with the principle of acting in a loving, caring manner, the next step is to realize that you have been choosing to allow your partner to dominate and control you. You may be surprised by this statement, but it's true. You've been allowing your spouse's responses or lack of the same to dictate what has been happening to your feelings, thoughts, and behaviors. You've let him/her do this. Now is the time to determine to respond in a positive, loving way regardless of what he/she does about it.

The formula for change and reactivating love feelings is quite simple— increase the positive and reduce the negative beliefs, thoughts, and behaviors. If there is something you want from your partner, be sure that it's stated in such a way that he/she will hear it and consider your request. (See *How to Change Your Spouse* by Gary Oliver and this author, chapter 3.)

Several other specific guidelines can be followed that may seem odd but are necessary. Consider this: You've probably been blaming your spouse for numerous things, and this has taken its toll upon your love feelings. But what if you could no longer blame him or her? What other reasons could you find for what is happening in your relationship? What other reasonable explanations could you discover? One wife shared her experience of doing this.

> When I had this suggestion I really resisted it. It didn't seem right or logical. And I guess a part of me didn't want to give up making him accountable. But I realized I didn't have much to lose. So I came up with this list:
>
> 1. It could be he really doesn't know how to do or give what I want and resists trying because who wants to fail?
> 2. I assumed he wasn't willing to learn what I want. I accused him of that.
> 3. I hate to admit it, but some of my approaches probably turned him off. I pushed him further away.
> 4. Perhaps he doesn't know how important this is to me and I can share it in a way he understands better.
>
> I hope all this works. Even if it doesn't, I won't feel so upset and I can say that I was willing to try something new.

People have asked me over the years, "How long, Norm? How long will this take?" No one can give you a time frame. I've seen the love return in months, but in some cases it takes years. Prayer and opening our lives completely for God to work within and on us is at the heart of the process. Change and restoration are possible. That's good news.

Notes

1. Karen Kayser, *When Love Dies* (New York: The Guilford Press, 1993).
2. Ibid., p. 6, adapted.
3. Ibid., pp. 20–24, adapted.
4. Charles Swindoll, *Come Before Winter* (Portland, Oreg.: Multnomah Books, 1985), p. 239.
5. Peter Krather with Bill Burns, *Affair Prevention* (New York: MacMillan Publishing Co., 1981), p. 68.
6. Kayser, *When Love Dies*, pp. 21–87, adapted.
7. From *How to Change Your Spouse (Without Ruining Your Marriage)*, © 1994 by H. Norman Wright and Gary Oliver, Ph.D. Published by Servant Publications, Box 8617, Ann Arbor, Michigan 48107. Used with permission, p. 209.
8. Adapted from Robert Paul Lieberman, Eugene Wheeler and Nancy Sanders, "Behavioral Therapy for Marital Disharmony: an Educational Approach," *Journal of Marriage and Family Counseling* (October 1976): 383–389.
9. Kayser, *When Love Dies*, p. 153, adapted.
10. Ibid., p. 152.
11. Lewis B. Smedes, *Forgive and Forget* (New York: HarperCollins, 1984), pp. 128–129.

—3—

WHAT MAKES A MARRIAGE WORK

They sat in my office, young and a bit anxious. They were both age twenty-two and fresh out of college. They had been engaged for three months, and the wedding was just six months away. The first question I asked them was: What are you expecting out of premarital counseling? What is it you want?

Their reply was similar to one I've heard from many couples over the years, but it had a different twist to it. They said, "We want to know what we need to do to make our marriage work and to stay married for the rest of our lives. We know about the importance of commitment and love. We believe in that. But what else can we do?" I've heard this before.

But then they added, "Since you've been counseling for many years and have listened to hundreds of couples, is there any way you could share with us now at this stage in our life and marriage what it takes married couples thirty-six years to learn? We've heard many older couples say they wished they knew back when they were first married what they know now after thirty or forty years of marriage. That's what we want to know now so we'll have a better chance at having a lasting and productive and fulfilling marriage. What do we need to know and what can we do?"

COUPLE STYLES

Since they had asked an important question, I decided to answer them with a question as well. I said, "Let me describe three different couples for you, and after I do I'd like to ask you a question to help answer your own question."

The Validating Couple

"The first couple work at their communication," I continued. "Occasionally they argue and disagree like all couples, but they deal with their differences before anger gets out of hand. They don't get into shouting matches but instead have 'conferences' in which each one has the opportunity to share his or her opinion.

"As they try to work toward understanding their partner, their goal is to work out a compromise. They can listen and hear their partner and can problem solve. There is a lot of mutual sharing. This type of couple has been called a validating couple because even when they don't agree with their partner's view or feelings, they accept them as valid."

The Volatile Couple

"The second couple," I continued, "is the kind you would hear fighting if they lived next door. They quarrel loudly, interrupt one another, and defend fiercely their own viewpoints. There is a lot of passion. They argue and debate minor issues that others would let pass. They don't really try to understand and empathize with their partner—their goal is to persuade. Rather than listen, they interrupt. They want to win.

"But couples like this are also very affectionate and loving in the same intense way. There's usually more laughter and affection than the validating couples experience. They express more positive feelings as well as negative ones, and they do this with ease. They are able to resolve their differences. They see themselves as equals, and believe marriage should emphasize strengths and individuality, not suppress them. Couples like this are called *volatile.*"

The Avoidant Couple

"The last couple," I concluded, "enjoys being together, and rarely do they fight. When disagreements arise, they tend to use time and distance to resolve the conflict. Rather than resolving differences, they tend to minimize their differences. And when they are discussed, nothing much seems to occur. They agree to disagree and avoid discussions they know will end up with nothing resolved. They don't put pressure on the other person to persuade them.

"Issues are resolved by avoiding or minimizing. They would rather focus on the positive—on what they love and value in marriage—and they accept the rest of the stuff. There isn't that much sharing or companionship in this kind of marriage. They like separateness and autonomy in their relationship. To an outsider, their interaction might appear shallow. They reflect some of the characteristics of what I call 'married singles'! All this is why they are called an *avoidant* couple."

WHICH STYLE IS THE MOST STABLE?

I then asked the couple the question "Having shared these three descriptions of couples, which would you say is a stable relationship?

They thought a minute and said, "Even though we're more like the second one, the volatile, it sounds like the first one, the validating couple, is the more stable one. The others could end up with some real problems."

I replied, "It's true the other two could get into serious difficulty. A *volatile* couple could end up being consumed by the constant quarreling. And unfortunately in some cases it could lead to violence. Some of the feelings they experience could really hurt their partner."

> An avoidant marriage could end up without the emotional con-
> nectedness the couple needs to hold their marriage together. And
> unresolved negative feelings could cause the relationship to
> deteriorate. They could become quite lonely, because neither
> fully knows nor understands his or her partner. Neither knows
> what's at the source of the partner's feelings, and when a major
> conflict does have to be faced some day, we might wonder
> whether they will have the skills they need to resolve it.[1]

Actually, the answer to the question of which type of marriage is the most stable is that all three of them can be stable. What makes the difference isn't so much the style of marriage you have as much as what happens within it. It's the amount of positive interaction you have. For your marriage to be stable you need at least five times as many positive as negative moments together! It's not whether you don't fight in a marriage, it's your ability to resolve the conflicts and have a high degree of positive rather than negative interaction.[2] If you have the five-to-one ratio, your marriage can last.

Volatile couples may vent a lot, but they spend more time being loving and positive. *Validators* have some tension but much more fun, love, and warmth. Even if avoidant couples don't show as much passion as others, they express less criticism and negatives. Your background, temperaments, and personalities have a lot to do with the style of marriage you develop. Positive thoughts and expressed feelings nourish both the marriage and the partners.[3]

Perhaps you are as surprised as the young couple in my office to hear that it's not so much the style of the marriage that determines its stability as the amount of positive interactions compared to negative. But it's true.

What about you? Does the positive overpower the negative or is it equal or less? Perhaps it would be beneficial for you to keep track for awhile. You might be surprised.

Accentuating the Positive

Perhaps you're like the couple in my office. I knew that they didn't want to leave what I said alone because they asked, "Norm, undoubtedly what you just shared with us is based on research. What was it that was described as positive and what was negative? I think it would help us to know the specifics."

They were right. Stable couples suggest numerous ways to express positive interactions in a marriage. And time and time again the Word of God admonishes us to behave in a positive and encouraging way. "And become useful and helpful and kind to one another, tenderhearted (compassionate, understanding, loving–hearted), forgiving one another [readily and freely], as God in Christ forgave you" (Eph. 4:32, *AMP*).

Paul also wrote:

> Clothe yourselves therefore, as God's own chosen ones (His own picked representatives), [who are] purified and holy and well–beloved [by God Himself, by putting on behavior marked by] tenderhearted pity and mercy, kind feeling, a lowly opinion of yourselves, gentle ways, [and] patience [which is tireless and long–suffering, and has the power to endure whatever comes, with good temper.] Be gentle and forbearing with one another and, if one has a difference (a grievance or complaint) against another, readily pardoning each other; even as the Lord has [freely] forgiven you, so must you also [forgive] (Col. 3:12,13, *AMP*).

Shared Interests

It's important to share interest in your partner as a person, to discover what he/she has experienced during the day, to uncover any upset feelings. This can involve listening and looking at each other—without glancing at the TV or the paper on your lap. It can mean listening without attempting to fix a problem unless asked to do so. If you're a man, it can mean giving more verbal responses and feedback when you listen, because women like to hear this so they will know you are listening. James 1:19 says to be "a ready listener" (*AMP*).

Showing Affection

Being consistently affectionate—and not just at those times when one is interested in sex—is a highly valued positive response. Sometimes nothing is shared verbally. It can be sitting side by side and touching gently or moving close enough that you barely touch while you watch the sun dipping over a mountain with reddish clouds capturing your attention. It could be reaching out and holding hands in public. It can be doing something thoughtful, unrequested and noticed only by your partner.

Or when your spouse has had a rough day, you may choose just to stroke her head, or rub his shoulders, instead of talking about it. Being so understood by your partner and having him or her meet your needs gives you the assurance that you have indeed married the right person.

Affection is demonstrated in many ways and displays. Years ago I heard the story of a couple who had been invited to a potluck dinner. The wife was not known for her cooking ability, but she decided to make a custard pie. As they drove to the dinner, they knew they were in trouble for they smelled the scorched crust. Then when they turned a corner, the contents of the pie shifted dramatically from one side of the pie shell to the other. He could see her anxiety rising by the moment.

When they arrived, they placed the pie on the dessert table. The guests were serving themselves salad and then went back for the main course. Just before they could move on to the desserts, the husband marched up to the table, looked over the number of homemade desserts and snatched up his wife's pie. As others looked at him, he announced, "There are so many desserts here and my wife so rarely makes my favorite dessert, I'm claiming this for myself. I ate light on all the other courses so now I can be a glutton."

And a glutton he was. Later his wife said, "He sat by the door eating what he could, mushing up the rest so no one else would bug him for a piece, and slipping chunks to the hosts' Rottweiler when no one was looking. He saw me looking at him and gave me a big wink. What he did made my evening. My husband, who doesn't always say much, communicated more love with what he did than with what any words could ever say."

Acts of Caring

Of course there are many other ways to take positive action, showing that you care. I raise flowers all year long, and I know Joyce enjoys seeing them inside the house. Often, after I've made the coffee, I cut her a rose and put it in a vase by her coffee cup. It's almost become automatic now, but the motivation is the same. And often, when I travel, Joyce slips a love note into my pants pocket.

Perhaps you're in the store and you see a favorite food your spouse enjoys and you buy it for him or her even if you hate it. Or you decide to stop at the store for an item and you call your spouse at home or at work to see if there's anything he or she wants or needs. You are "other" thinking rather than "self" thinking. You follow through with the scriptural teaching in Ephesians 4:32 (*NIV*), "Be kind and compassionate to one another."

An act of caring can be a phone call to ask if your partner has a prayer request. Acts of caring can mean remembering special dates and anniversaries without being reminded. I am amazed at the number of wives who have been deeply hurt by their husbands over the years because they did not remember anniversaries or even birthdays.

And their excuses are so lame. I've heard, "I just didn't remember" and "I need to be reminded" and "We just didn't do that in our family." That's all such responses are—excuses! If the husband is sitting in my counseling office, I simply ask him if he forgets to go to work or to get involved in his hobby. Reluctantly he says no, and I go on to let him know that I believe he is capable of learning something new that will benefit both his life and his wife's. We then talk about how he will do it. We don't accept excuses when it is obvious that change can occur.

Showing Appreciation and Empathy

Another positive is being appreciative. This means going out of your way to notice all the little positive things your partner does and letting him or her know you appreciate them. It also means focusing on the positive experiences and dwelling upon those rather than the negative (more will be said about this later). Working toward agreement and appreciating the other's perspective is important. Compliments convey appreciation, but they need to be balanced between what persons do and who they are. Affirmations based on personal qualities are rare, but highly appreciated.

Showing genuine concern for your spouse when you notice he or she is upset builds unity and intimacy in a relationship. You may not be able to do anything, but sharing your desire to do so may be all that is necessary. When your partner shares a problem with you, don't relate a similar problem you once had, tell him what to do, crack jokes to cheer him up, or ask how he got into that problem in the first place. Instead, listen, put your arm around him, show that you understand, and let him know it's all right for him to feel and act the way he does.

I'm sure you've heard the word *empathy* time and time again. This is the feeling of being with another person both emotionally and intellectually. It's viewing life through your spouse's eyes, feeling as he or she feels, and hearing his or her story through your mate's perceptions.

In marriage you have a choice to respond with empathy, sympathy, or apathy. Sympathy is being overinvolved in the emotions of your spouse. It can actually undermine your emotional strength. Apathy means you couldn't care less. There are no in-betweens.

Empathy includes rapport—knowing how your spouse would feel in most situations without him or her having to explain. You'll experience something together at the same time through the eyes of your partner.

Accepting each other for who you are and what you say is a positive.

Acceptance means letting your spouse know that even though you don't agree with what he or she is saying, you are willing to hear him or her out. It means freeing your partner from being molded into the fantasy that you want him or her to be. It's more than tolerance. It's saying, "You and I are different in many ways. It's all right for you to be you and for me to be me. We are stronger together than we are separately, as we learn to complement one another." This doesn't mean spouses won't help to change each other—that's inevitable. But the purpose for which it's done, and the method, makes a world of difference.

The Lighter Side

Having a sense of humor and being able to laugh, joke, and have fun gives balance to the serious side of marriage. Some of what you laugh at will be private, and some will be shared with others. Having a sense of humor means you are able to laugh at yourself (even if it sometimes takes awhile!), and the two of you can laugh together. Sometimes the best memories are some of those hilarious incidents that happen even though your partner didn't think it was so funny at the time.

Several years ago while speaking at a family camp at Forest Home, California, such an event happened to Joyce and me. We were staying in a nice cabin, and since I'm an early riser I went down to the dining hall for an early breakfast. Joyce arose a little later and didn't eat a large breakfast, knowing that I would bring her back some fruit and a muffin. I entered the cabin and was just about ready to go into the bedroom with her food, when the door of the bathroom was flung open. Joyce, fresh out of the shower, said, "Don't go in there! It's still there! Don't take my food in there!"

I was shocked and said, "What!? What's in there?!"

"In there!" she said again, almost in tears by now. "It's still in the bedroom. It was terrible. And don't you dare laugh. It wasn't funny!" I still didn't know what she was talking about, but saying to a husband, "Don't you dare laugh!" is like a subtle invitation that may get played out later.

Finally, she calmed down and told me what happened. She had been resting in bed drinking her coffee when she decided to reach down and pick up her slippers. She found one, lifted it up, and then thrust her hand under the bed to find the other one. Now, Forest Home was using new humane mouse-traps that consisted of a six-by-six-inch piece of cardboard with an extremely sticky substance on it. When a mouse stuck in it, it was stuck permanently and would eventually die. Well...you can guess what happened. Not only did Joyce put her hand directly on the goo substance, but it also contained a bloated dead mouse! It was gross! (I have a picture of it.) As she said, she went ballistic with screams, trying to dislodge this disgusting creature from her hand.

As Joyce was telling me all this, she was shaking her hand and demonstrating how she had tried to dislodge the mouse from her hand. And the more she did this the funnier it got. I was biting the inside of my mouth to keep from smiling and all the time remembering those fateful words "Don't you dare laugh. It's not funny." I think she saw my struggle, because with an exaggerated pout she looked at me and said again, slowly, *"It's not funny."*

That's all it took. I was a dead man and I knew it. I laughed until the tears rolled down my face. I did take the mouse out and get rid of it. I also told Joyce that I would have gone into hysterics as well if that had happened to me, and that she had every right to be upset. After several hugs, she said, "I guess it was pretty funny at that." Now it's one of our favorite stories.

We also have many funny memories in which I was the source of the amusement. Just ask Joyce sometime and you'll hear a whole list of them.

A related positive in marriage is the sense of shared joy.[4] You share your partner's excitement and delight and you want your partner to be aware of what you're experiencing as well. Joy is a sense of gladness, not necessarily happiness. It's also a command from Scripture: We are to "rejoice with those who rejoice" (Rom. 12:15, *NIV*).

Avoiding the "Takens"

Another positive is never becoming complacent or taking one another for granted. A friend of mine described it in this way:

> People in long-term marriages tend to take each other for granted. The most common of the "takens" include:
>
> You will always be here for me.
>
> You will always love me.
>
> You will always be able to provide for me.
>
> You will always be the same.
>
> We will always be together.
>
> Making these assumptions in a marriage is living more in fantasyland than on reality ridge. People who take things for granted are seldom appreciative of the everyday blessings in their lives. After a time, they come to believe life owes them these little gifts. They seldom say thank you for anything.
>
> When you take someone for granted you demean him or her. You send the unspoken message, You are not worth much to me. You also rob this person of the gift of human appreciation. And to be loved and appreciated gives all of us a reason to live each day. When that gift is withdrawn or denied over the years, our spirits wither and die. People may endure this hardship and stay married forever, but they are only serving a sentence. In long-

term marriages where one or both spouses are continually taken for granted, a wall of indifference arises between husband and wife. The longer the marriage, the higher the wall and the greater the human isolation. The way out of this woodpile is simple but crucial:

Start saying thank you and showing appreciation for anything and everything.

Be more consciously tuned in to what is going on around you.

Become more giving and affirming.

Specialize in the many little things that mean a lot: Bring each other flowers, take long walks in the country, lie on the floor in front of the fireplace, prepare breakfast in bed for each other, hold hands in public and walk in the rain, send caring and funny cards to each other in the mail, buy each other small gifts for no apparent reason.

Remember: A thirty-five year marriage does not guarantee year number thirty-six. Take nothing for granted just because you have it today.[5]

Keep in mind that in a healthy marriage...

You look out for "number 2" rather than number 1.

You energize your spouse rather than drain energy from him or her.

You eliminate blaming and shaming from the marriage.

You are willing to learn from your partner.

You end your disagreements with a feeling of resolve.

You feel better after a disagreement.[6]

These are just some of the positives that keep a marriage alive. Much more will be shared about this throughout the book. But what about you? On a scale of zero to ten, how would you rate the presence of these positives in your own marriage (zero being nonexistent and ten being super abundance)? How would your spouse rate these? (In the appendix you will find a marriage assessment form that will enable you to take a fresh look at your marriage.)

DESTRUCTIVE FORCES IN MARRIAGE

At the same time that we measure positives, it is helpful to be just as knowledgeable about the factors that could destroy a relationship. Revelation 6 portrays the four horses of the Apocalypse: a white, red, pale, and black horse. This description has been used to describe destructive forces in marriage. They fit many unhappy marriages, even with their unique variations, because they follow basically the same downward spiral before they come to a state of disintegration and the marriage is overcome by negativity. When we see these behaviors in a couple's relationship, it's possible to predict with a safe amount of accuracy which marriages will most likely end in divorce. That's a bit frightening, isn't it? Especially if your own marriage fits the profile. The good news is that if a couple identifies this downward spiral, corrective action can be taken to stop it. I've seen this occur time after time over the years.

The four horsemen of the Apocalypse correspond with four of the most disastrous ways a couple could interact in order to destroy the marriage. These are *criticism, contempt, defensiveness,* and *stonewalling.*

As each of these behaviors becomes more a part of the marriage it seems that a couple's attention is then diverted from the positive to the negative. And soon they're consumed by the negative. As each of these attitudes or behaviors gains a foothold in the relationship, it opens the door for the next horseman to step through and enhance the destruction. Actually these four are contaminates. They infect the relationship with a toxic substance that gradually erodes the feelings of love.

Riding the Critical Horse

All couples will voice complaints from time to time. That's normal, and complaints can be voiced in a way that a spouse will hear them and not be defensive. For example, instead of focusing upon what annoys you, talk more about what you would *appreciate* your spouse doing. Your partner is much more likely to hear you and consider your request if you ride the horse of appreciation instead of the steed of criticism. Talking about what you don't like just reinforces the possibility of its continuing with an even greater intensity. The principle of pointing toward what you would like also conveys to your partner your belief that he/she is capable of doing what you have requested. Doing this consistently, along with giving praise and appreciation when your spouse complies, will bring about a change.

I've seen this in children as well as adults. The power of praise cannot be underestimated. I've also seen this principle work in raising our golden retriever, Sheffield—not that I'm comparing people to dogs. Sheffield was trained in the basics by the time he was four months old, and now he brings in the paper, takes items back and forth to Joyce and me, "answers" the phone and brings it to me, and picks up items off the floor and puts them in the trash. All it took was ignoring the times when he didn't do it right, and giving praise and hugs when he came through.

I don't think people are much different in this respect. Affirming and encouraging responses can literally change a person's life, because we do want and need others to believe in us. An unusual example of this is found in the Babemba tribe in southern Africa. When one of the tribal members has acted irresponsibly, he or she is taken to the center of the village. Everyone in the village stops work and gathers in a large circle around the person. In turn, each person, regardless of age, speaks to the person and recounts the good things he has done in his lifetime. All the positive incidents in the person's life, plus his good attributes, strengths, and kindnesses, are recalled with accuracy and detail. Not one word about his problem behaviors is even mentioned.

This ceremony, which sometimes lasts several days, isn't complete until every positive expression has been given by those assembled. The person is literally flooded by positives. When the people are finished, the person is welcomed back into the tribe. Can you imagine how all this makes persons feel about themselves? Can you imagine their desire to continue to reflect those positive qualities? Perhaps a variation of this is needed in marriages and families today.

Criticism is the initial negative response that opens the door for the other destructive responses to follow. Criticism is different from complaining in that it attacks the other person's personality and character, usually with blame. Most criticisms are overgeneralized ("You always...") and personally accusing (the word "you" is central). A great deal of criticism comes in the form of blame, with the word "should" being included.

Criticism can be hidden under the camouflage of joking and humor. And when confronted about it, a person will avoid responsibility by saying, "Hey, I was just joking." It reminds me of the passage in Proverbs that says, "Like a madman who casts firebrands, arrows, and death, so is the man who deceives his neighbor and then says, Was I not joking?" (Prov. 26:18,19, *AMP*).

Faultfinding is a common form of criticism. It's a favorite response of the perfectionistic spouse. (For assistance in handling this problem in a marriage, see chapter 11 of *How to Change Your Spouse*, by Gary Oliver and this author.)

Criticism is usually destructive, but it's interesting to hear critics say they're just trying to remold their partners into better persons by offering some "constructive" criticism. But too often criticism does not construct; it demolishes. It doesn't nourish a relationship; it poisons. And often the presentation is like this description: "There is one who speaks rashly like the thrusts of a sword" (Prov. 12:18, *NASB*).

Criticism that is destructive accuses, tries to make the other feel guilty, intimidates, and is often an outgrowth of personal resentment.

Criticism comes in many shapes and sizes. You've heard of "zingers," those lethal, verbal guided missiles. A zinger comes at you with a sharp point and a dull barb that catches the flesh as it goes in. The power of these sharp, caustic statements is seen when you realize that one zinger can undo twenty acts of kindness. That's right, *twenty*.

A zinger has the power to render many positive acts meaningless. Once a zinger has landed, the effect is similar to a radioactive cloud that settles on an area of what used to be prime farm land. The land is so contaminated by the radioactivity that, even though seeds are scattered and plants are planted, they fail to take root. Subsequently they die out or are washed away by the elements. It takes decades for the contamination to dissipate. The kind acts of loving words following the placement of a zinger find a similar hostile soil. It may take hours before there is a receptivity or positive response to your positive overtures.[7]

Another form of criticism is called *invalidation* and is often the cause of marital distress. When invalidation is present in a marriage, it destroys the effect of *validation*, as well as the friendship relationship of marriage. Sometimes couples get along and maintain their relationships without sufficient validation, but they cannot handle continual invalidation. This is yet another example of one negative comment destroying twenty acts of kindness.[8]

Invalidation is like a slow, fatal disease that, once established in a relationship, spreads and destroys the positive feelings. As one wife said, "The so-called friend I married became my enemy with his unexpected attacks. I felt demeaned, put-down, and my self-esteem slowly crumbled. I guess that's why our fights escalated so much. I had to fight to survive." To keep love and your marriage alive, keep the criticism out of it.

Instead of just being critical when a problem occurs, perhaps you could respond like the pilot in this story:

> Bob Hoover, a famous test pilot and frequent performer at air shows, was returning to his home in Los Angeles from an air show in San Diego. As described in the magazine *Flight Operations*, at 300 feet in the air, both engines suddenly stopped. By deft maneuvering he managed to land the plane, but it was badly damaged although nobody was hurt.
>
> Hoover's first act after the emergency landing was to inspect the airplane's fuel. Just as he suspected, the World War II propeller plane he had been flying had been fueled with jet fuel rather than gasoline.
>
> Upon returning to the airport, he asked to see the mechanic who had serviced his plane. The young man was sick with the agony of his mistake. Tears streamed down his face as Hoover approached. He had just caused the loss of a very expensive plane and could have caused the loss of three lives as well.
>
> You can imagine Hoover's anger. One could anticipate the tongue-lashing that this proud and precise pilot would unleash for the carelessness. But Hoover didn't scold the mechanic; he didn't even criticize him. Instead, he put his big arm around the

man's shoulder and said, "To show you I'm sure that you'll never do this again, I want you to service my F51 tomorrow."[9]

Lobbing Shells of Contempt

The next step down the path of destruction is contempt—the intent to insult or psychologically abuse your spouse. That sounds harsh, doesn't it? But that is what happens. It's like using a mortar in a battle to lob shells into the enemy lines. But in a marriage you're lobbing insults into the person you promised to love. Negative thoughts and negative statements abound, and nothing is sacred. Name-calling, nonverbal actions, and mocking are all part of the pattern.

The Danger of Defensiveness

Contempt brings to the forefront the third and fourth elements of destruction in a marriage—*defensiveness* and *stonewalling*. These are natural protective responses intended to diffuse the attacks coming from the outside. Defensive statements are usually viewed as excuses, and often they are. Frequently they're accompanied by a counterattack. The greater the degree of defensiveness between a couple, the less the amount of emotional intimacy. Even though your partner's attack may be grossly exaggerated, unreasonable, and unfair, defensiveness and stonewalling are not your only options. Let's consider what you might be able to do instead.

REDEEMING DESTRUCTIVE FORCES

Realize that not all criticism is bad. Consider what God's Word has to say about criticism. "It is a badge of honor to accept valid criticism" (Prov. 25:12, *TLB*). "What a shame—yes, how stupid!—to decide before knowing the facts!" (18:13, *TLB*). "Don't refuse to accept criticism; get all the help you can" (23:12, *TLB*). "A man who refuses to admit his mistakes can never be successful. But if he confesses and forsakes them, he gets another chance" (28:13, *TLB*). Don't automatically assume that all negative criticism is invalid.

Evaluate the criticism for validity. I realize that this step may be easier said than done. Looking for value in destructive criticism may be like searching for a needle in a haystack. But you must ask yourself "What can I learn from this experience? Is there a grain of truth in what I am hearing to which I need to respond?" Asking questions like these will shift you from the position of the defendant in a relationship to that of an investigator. However unfair your spouse's attack, disregard the negative statements. Give your partner permission to exaggerate. Eventually the exaggerated statements will blow away like chaff and only the truth will remain. Keep searching for the grain of truth. Try to identify the real cause for his or her critical attack.

Clarify the root problem. Try to determine precisely what your spouse thinks you have done, or not done, that is bothering him or her. It's important that you understand the criticism from the other person's point of view. Ask specific questions such as "Will you please elaborate on the main point?" or "Can you give me a specific example?" Suppose your wife says, "You're the most inconsiderate person in the world!" That's a very general statement. Challenge her to identify specific ways you have acted inconsiderately. Ask for examples from your relationship. Keep digging until the root is exposed.

Think about the charge. At times, the process of investigating accusations and criticisms may overwhelm you with anger, confusion, or frustration. In the rush of these emotions, your mind may pull a disappearing act—it may go blank! You need time to think before you respond. How can you do this?

First I need to warn you against how *not* to do it. Don't ask "Can I take a minute to think about this?" Don't ask anyone's permission to take time to think. Also, don't say "Are you sure you are seeing this situation accurately?" This question gives your spouse the opportunity to make another value judgment on the issue. You are vesting him or her with unneeded power.

It is better to say "I'm going to take a few minutes to think this over" or "That's an interesting perspective. I need to think about it." Then ask yourself "What is the main point he is trying to make? What does he want to happen as a result of our discussion?" Sometimes it is helpful to clarify that point with your mate by asking "What would you like to be different about me as a result of our discussion? I'm really interested in knowing."

Respond positively and confidently. Once the central issue has been exposed, confidently explain your actions rather than withering defensively under the attack. I think people who criticize others expect their victims to be defensive, even though these critics sometimes say, "I wish they wouldn't be so defensive when I make a suggestion [their word for a critical demand!]." Critical people say they want their spouses to be nondefensive, but they are often shaken to the core when someone stands up to their criticism.

One man told me that he wished his wife wouldn't be defensive. I asked him, "How would you respond if you criticized her and she *wasn't* defensive?"

He looked at me, laughed a little, and said, "I guess I'd faint dead away."

I said, "You mean you expect her to be defensive, yet you wish she weren't?"

"Yes," he answered after a thoughtful pause. "I guess that sounds a bit strange. The very thing I want her not to do is what I expect her to do. I wonder if my attitude toward her is helping create her defensiveness."

Let's listen in on one husband's attempt to respond to his wife's criticism positively and confidently instead of defensively. The couple is talking in my counseling office. Sandra is bothered because Jim isn't as sociable as she is.

He keeps putting her off when she tries to get him involved with other people. Sandra has a legitimate concern, but Jim also has a legitimate reason for not wanting to be involved, which he has never shared with her. Notice the communication process:

Sandra (quite angry): I'm really fed up. I've asked you time and time again about getting together with other people and you continue to refuse. I'm beginning to believe you don't like people. You're like a hermit. You just sit home and read.

Jim (good-naturedly): Am I really that bad? A hermit?

Sandra (with a slight laugh): You're much worse than that. I was giving you the benefit of the doubt.

Jim: Well, can you be more specific?

Sandra: You know when you're being antisocial. It happens at church and it happens when we're with my relatives.

Jim: I'm not sure about that. Can you give me an example?

Sandra: I can give you several. Last week when we were going out for dinner, I suggested that we invite John and Heather to go with us. You were upset because we hadn't planned it out beforehand. You have this thing about planning social activities weeks ahead. I wish you could be more flexible.

Jim: Are you saying that you'd like me to be more flexible? You want me to loosen up and be willing to do things without all that planning?

Sandra: That would sure help. I'd like to see you stop being so rigid. We would both be happier.

Jim: And you thought I was being antisocial the other night because I didn't want to invite John and Heather to join us on the spur of the moment.

Sandra: Yes, but that's just one example. It happens a lot.

Jim: Well, I guess that's something I can work on. I would also enjoy more of a social life, but I need more time to adjust to getting together with others.

Sandra: You've never told me that before. I didn't realize our social activities with others were such a difficulty for you.

Even though Sandra, in her frustration, led off the dialogue with an attacking, accusatory statement, Jim didn't let it throw him. And that's the point. You can respond in a healthy, positive way regardless of the other person's style of criticism. Jim responded in such a way that Sandra felt he was hearing her. And Sandra gained a deeper understanding of their personality differences.

Agree with the criticism. No matter how hostile or destructive the criticism may be, agree with it to a certain extent. By doing so you will communicate to your spouse that he or she has been heard and that you are not defensive.

For years I have used a book with my counselees called *When I Say "NO," I Feel Guilty*. One of the two chapters I use is on a technique designed to handle another person's criticism without becoming defensive. This is called "fogging."

If a husband criticizes his wife as not being adventuresome or wanting to go out much, she could respond with, "You know, you're probably right. I'm not that adventuresome." When a response like this is given without defensiveness or counterattack, where else does the potential argument have to go except... nowhere! There is nothing to fight against because there is no resistance.

Manuel Smith describes this response as similar to a fog bank. Fog in our area of the country can be so thick at times that you can't see anything ten feet away. Sometimes it seems heavy and sloppy. But if you were to throw a rock at the fog bank, it would just keep on going. It wouldn't bounce off or bounce back at you. There's no resistance.

And when a spouse criticizes you, his or her criticism has no effect when you don't participate with either defense or counterattack.

When you fog you will discover that you listen in a new way. You hear what was said and respond to it at face value. It keeps you from being defensive because you have quit thinking in terms of absolutes. You are now thinking in terms of probabilities, such as "There is even a small probability they could be correct."

There are actually three methods of dealing with put-downs: agreeing with truth, agreeing in principle, and agreeing with the odds.

When you agree with truth it means you listen carefully for any seed of truth in the criticism and only the truth. If there is a put-down or some implied derogatory remark, ignore that. You can agree with the possibility that something is true.

> *Wife:* You're late again. I can never depend on you to be home on time.
> *Husband:* Wow—It's past seven. Time got away from me. You're right. I'm late.

An example of agreeing with a principle is seen in this discussion:

> *Wife:* It's going to be expensive to hire someone else to do all the tree trimming this year if you're not going to do it.
> *Husband:* That's true. It will cost more to have someone else do this for us.

Some spouses don't come out clear and straight with their criticisms. They try to be subtle and sneak in with their remarks. They use what I call sideswipe comments. An example would be the husband who says, "Most wives I know take time and fix up for their husbands before they come home at night." Instead of responding with "Are you saying I don't?" or "I fix up when I'm able to do so" or "*Now*, what are you criticizing me about?" there is an alternate response. One wife replies to such a comment, "Well, that's good that they do and it's nice that you notice that." This puts the responsibility back in the other person's lap to state a direct request. Your response will disarm your attacker and you will no longer have a real opponent.

There is a skill and process called *penetrating listening*. It's like some of our sophisticated weaponry used in war in which the bomb or missile penetrates deep within the defensive structure before it explodes. It works because it is not put off by the initial defense, but penetrates to where it will have the greatest effect. Listening that can penetrate by going beyond the anger or contempt in a partner's voice may pick up the core concern that is often disguised in the heat of a quarrel. If your listening is nondefensive, you will be less likely to respond defensively, and when you don't contribute any fuel to the fire, it soon dies out.

The Stonewalling Stage
When criticism, contempt, and defensiveness become permanent residents in a marriage, they strangle the flow of communication. And communication is to a marriage what blood is to the body. Without it, you die. *Stonewalling* is one of the many descriptions of this last and worst stage.

At this state, both partners may feel like they're talking to a brick wall. There is little or no response. The loudest sound is silence, and the message it imparts is distance and disapproval. It's a method used more by husbands than by wives. The silent retreat irritates a wife and sends her the message that he doesn't love her. Men avoid conflict in marriage more than wives, and it upsets them more physiologically. When this condition becomes chronic it usually sounds the death cry for a marriage even when just one partner employs this tactic.[10]

It's difficult to maintain the five-to-one ratio of positive to negative when the four horsemen are racing through your marriage. The minute any of them begin to invade your marriage, it should be viewed as an unwelcome guest and exited. (Again I would urge you to read *How to Change Your Spouse* by Oliver and Wright for detailed assistance on what you can do. I will recommend this many times as a practical companion volume to this text. Another excellent resource is *What Your Mother Never Told You & What Your Father Didn't Know* by John Gray [HarperCollins].)

If these negatives have become a part of your marriage routine, are you ready to do (not try, but *do*) something new? Throughout this book, as well as others recommended, you will find better ways of responding. After all, if what you're doing now isn't working, why keep on doing it? There *is* a better way.

NOTES

1. John Gottman, *Why Marriages Succeed or Fail* (New York: Simon & Schuster, 1994), pp. 41–47, adapted.
2. Ibid., p. 57, adapted.
3. Ibid., adapted.
4. Ibid., pp. 58–61, adapted.
5. Jim Smoke, *Facing 50* (Nashville: Thomas Nelson, 1994), pp. 40–41.
6. Paul Pearsall, *The Ten Laws of Lasting Love* (New York: Simon & Schuster, 1993), pp. 298–299, adapted.
7. Clifford Notarius and Howard Markman, *We Can Work It Out* (New York: G. P. Putnam's Sons, 1993), p. 28, adapted.
8. Ibid., pp. 123–124, adapted.
9. Dale Carnegie, *How to Win Friends and Influence People* (New York: Pocket Books, 1936), pp. 41–42.
10. Gottman, *Why Marriages Succeed or Fail*, pp. 70–102, adapted.

–4–

A VISION FOR YOUR MARRIAGE

"I had a dream," my client said. "It seemed like a realistic dream at the time. I could almost see what was going to happen in the future. I was sure it was within reach. June and I both had so much to offer. We were in love but highly realistic. We were convinced that our marriage was made in heaven, and for awhile it seemed to be. But then that dream we had when we married began to fade and get a bit fuzzy. It wasn't at the forefront of our thoughts anymore. It was there, but so were a lot of other things in our lives. All too soon we were into routines and ruts. Our marriage wasn't fresh anymore. And here we are, fifteen years later, wondering what happened. Are we just like everyone else with a lackluster marriage? It feels like we're just drifting and too often on the edge of a whirlpool."

I've heard it many times in my counseling office—a marriage ending up where the couple never wanted it to be. So many marry with the belief, "We're getting married and because we're Christians and we love each other, we have what it takes for our marriage to work and to be what we want it to be."

But if I press them and ask "What do you really want your marriage to be?" the reply is often generalized and vague. When a couple responds "Marriage isn't what we thought it would be," only general disappointment is being voiced. What they really wanted from the marriage is vague, and that's a big part of the problem.

DRIFTING OR DREAMING?

In one of his books originally titled *The Drifting Marriage*, a fellow counselor describes so well what happens to marriages. Listen to this description and ask yourself if it describes anyone you know.

> Drifting is one of the most common forms of marital failure. In fact, I would venture to say that the majority of those couples found in our churches from Sunday to Sunday have marriages which are "adrift." Just think about that for a moment. Look across the pews. Would you guess that a majority of your friends have marriages that are in trouble? Probably not. Neither would they.
>
> Drifting. Not only is it the most common form of marital failure, it is also the most dangerous. It is subtle. It is quiet. It is non-offensive. It sounds no alarms. It just gradually creeps into our lives. And then it destroys.
>
> Step by step, the emotional deadness sneaks up on us as we move further and further away from our mates. The appearance of "all is well" is our placard. We fail to see the absence of real caring. Why should we see it? We have our preoccupations to keep us busy. The absence of emotional pain is accepted as a sign that everything is "fine." We have grown accustomed to the way things are.[1]

Drifting occurs because of a lack of purpose, the absence of personal and marital goals, and a vacuum where a sense of vision ought to be.

Do you have a vision for your marriage? Have you established specific goals for your marriage that you would like to achieve? Have you and your spouse discussed and evaluated where your marriage is and where you want it to be three to six months from now? I asked this of a couple in counseling and I received an interesting reply. "Norm, we don't even know what you're talking about. What do you mean a 'vision' for your marriage? And how can we think of what we want three to six months from now when we're just trying to survive on a day-to-day basis?"

Although many people feel that way, lasting marriages not only have the characteristics we have already described; they have senses of vision for their marriages as well.

VISION FOR THE JOURNEY

Here is my premise for this chapter: Unless you have a clear and precise understanding of where you are heading in your marriage, the probability of a successful journey is limited.

In the *King James Version* of Proverbs 29:18 there is a statement that is a foundation for a successful marriage. It reads, "Where there is no vision, the people perish." A paraphrase of this is "Where there is no vision, a marriage relationship stops growing and begins to crumble." Unless you as a couple have a clear understanding of where you are heading, the probability of a successful marriage is limited, and drifting could lead you to the driveway of a divorce court.

Having a vision for anything is like having a dream. But you know, sometimes dreamers are scoffed at. Joseph was a dreamer and was subject to ridicule from his brothers (see Genesis 37). Sometimes dreams fade if we receive too much negative reaction. Sometimes we start to disbelieve our own dreams and become content to remain right where we are.

But dreams can also be contagious. Do you remember the dream of the man that day in 1963 who stood in front of thousands of people and cried out again and again, "I have a dream"? His dream was for justice and equality for black people. He never gave up on his dream, and the dream of Martin Luther King Jr. is now part of mainstream American consciousness. Dr. David Seamands, who heard Dr. King cry out his dream that day, says simply, "That day I learned the awesome power of an awe-inspiring dream, and I returned home lifted and encouraged."

> The diminutive Albanian woman we today know as Mother Teresa was nothing more than average early in her life. Her colleagues in the convent have remarked that she was nothing special as a student, as a leader or as a woman seeking to please God. However, after years of prayer and a spirit broken by Him, she emerged as a figure to be reckoned with, moved beyond complacency to a deep compassion for the poorest of the poor. Summoning courage unfamiliar to her, she requested that her religious order permit her to initiate a ministry in India to care for those who were so sick that no other people or organizations bothered to care for them.
>
> Why risk her life and the few human comforts she knew to begin a life of even greater sacrifice and ignominy? Because she felt a special calling from God to reach out to "love the unlovable." She could very easily have continued her ministry as a nun, teaching in schools, leading young women to consider a relationship with Christ, even directing some special students toward a vocational ministry. Nobody would have questioned her love for God, her commitment to His Kingdom, her selflessness as a nun.
>
> Yet, she knew that God had reached out to her with a special vision for what she could do to impact people's lives for His

glory. And what an impact she has had, one that exceeds her innate intellect, courage and physical strength. She has felt compelled to change the lives of people because God has given her a special vision for outreach.[2]

The prophet said it for us: "Your old men will dream dreams, your young men will see visions" (Joel 2:28, *NASB*). When you have vision, you may find yourself battling upstream, but you'll experience God's blessing and His presence as you cooperate with His work in your life. When you see things as they could be, especially in your marriage, you won't let the odds overwhelm you. When you see things as they could be, you'll recognize obstacles, but you won't dwell on them.

DESCRIBING THE VISION

In seminars I've had people ask me: What do you mean by a vision, especially having a vision for your marriage? I tell them that there are many ways to think about vision. Vision could be described as *foresight,* with the significance of possessing a keen awareness of current circumstances and possibilities, and of the value of learning from the past.

Vision can also be described as *seeing the invisible and making it visible.* It's having a picture held in your mind of the way things could or should be in the days ahead.

Vision is also *a portrait of conditions that don't yet exist.* It's being able to focus more on the future than getting bogged down with the past or present. Vision is the process of creating a better future with God's empowerment and direction.[3]

Here are some other thoughts describing what vision means:

> Vision is the dominant force that controls your life and it impacts the choices you make as a person and a couple. It's what your thoughts lean toward when you are not focused on something else.
>
> It can direct the type of relationships and friendships that you form. It's also what you pray about as you seek God's will.[4]

Vision as a Magnet
A vision should be like a magnet that draws us out of the past and into the blessings of the future. I thought of this recently while watching the popular film *Dances with Wolves.* I was greatly intrigued with the animal scenes. During the stampede scene there are hundreds of buffalo thundering across the plain. At one point a buffalo appears to be charging directly at an Indian

boy. As I watched, I wondered, *How did the filmmakers get that buffalo to do what they wanted?*

I later discovered in a magazine article that a great deal of time had been invested in the scene with that one buffalo. In order to get the buffalo to cooperate, they conditioned it by feeding it Oreo cookies. It wasn't long before the animal would practically jump through a hoop to get to those round, chocolate, cream-filled cookies. So for the stampede scene they placed a pile of Oreos next to the Indian boy (and out of sight of the camera), and the cookies drew the buffalo in the right direction just like a powerful magnet.

Vision as Visualizing

One of the current figures in the field of effective management and character development is Stephen Covey. He encourages leaders to begin each day with a mental picture of the end of their lives as the criteria for everything they choose to do each day.

If you've ever followed golf you'll recognize the name of Jack Nicklaus as one of the legends of this sport. In order to accomplish what he wants in his sport he envisions what he wants to happen as well as how he will make it happen. Nicklaus writes:

> I never hit a shot, even in practice, without having a very sharp, in-focus picture of it in my head. First I "see" the ball where I want it to finish, nice and white and sitting up high on the bright green grass. Then the scene quickly changes and I "see" the ball going there: its path, trajectory, and shape, even its behavior on the landing. Then there's a sort of fade-out, and the next scene shows me making the kind of swing that will turn the previous image into reality.[5]

Here's what Chuck Swindoll says about vision:

> Vision is the ability to see God's presence, to perceive God's power, to focus on God's plan in spite of the obstacles....Vision is the ability to see above and beyond the majority. Vision is perception—reading the presence and power of God into one's circumstances. I sometimes think of vision as looking at life through the lens of God's eyes, seeing situations as He sees them. Too often we see things not as they are, but as we are. Think about that. Vision has to do with looking at life with a divine perspective, reading the scene with God in clear focus.
>
> Whoever wants to live differently in "the system" must correct his or her vision.[6]

Vision's Uniqueness

Vision is specific, detailed, customized, distinctive, sometimes time–related, and measurable. In marriage, vision is a way of describing its activity and development.[7] The vision you have for your marriage may be uniquely different from another person's. Having a vision for your marriage is having a realistic dream for what you, your spouse, and your marriage can become under God's direction. And we need to seek what God wants for us and our marriages, because without His wisdom what we achieve may be out of His will. We need His wisdom, because "The Lord knows the thoughts of man; he knows that they are futile" (Ps. 94:11, *NIV*).

Dr. Charles Stanley talks about vision for the Christian life:

> The Lord often shows us a general picture of what we are to do—and that broad overview tends to intimidate us and scare us. We need to realize that the Lord doesn't leave us with a giant goal or a great plan—He provides direction for all of the small steps that are necessary for getting to the big goal.
>
> Ask the Lord to show you the first step that you need toward the goal. Recognize that it will be only a step. Be patient with yourself and with God's working in you. Do what He shows you to do with all your strength, might, and talent. And then look for the second step that He leads you to take.
>
> The Lord doesn't catapult us into greatness; He grows us into spiritual maturity.
>
> He stretches us slowly so that we don't break.
>
> He expands our vision slowly so that we can take in all of the details of what He desires to accomplish.
>
> He causes us to grow slowly so that we stay balanced.
>
> The unfolding of God's plan for our lives is a process. Expect to be engaged in that process for the rest of your life.[8]

And this is true for a marriage as well.

FROM DREAM TO REALITY

What we need is vision that employs action.

> This power of vision to fulfill needs and turn dreams into reality is what I call action–vision. Action–vision is an image of desired results that inspires us to action. It's more than just a snapshot from our hope chest. It's a visualization of the possibilities, the probabilities, and the process of making things happen.

Action-vision doesn't mean developing a tunnel vision of what we think our life should be like and then feeling we've missed the mark when it doesn't happen. Instead, it's recognizing the desires of our heart and being actively involved in the process of seeing them become reality or being willing to revamp the blueprints. In this mode of living, God's will is not some elusive dream, but a daily reality. It's a method of setting direction for the future that allows us to live fully today.[9]

How does all this apply to your marriage? What do you do? How do you do it? Where do you begin? A goal makes a dream become a reality, especially when you break down your long-range goals into short-range. For some it is easier to talk about having goals for their marriages rather than creating visions for them. The purpose of a vision or a goal is to bring change to your marriage.

Change as Positive

The word *change* means to make different, to give a different course or direction, to replace one thing with another, to make a shift from one to another, to undergo transformation or transition. Some see change as negative or threatening. I've even had some couples say, "Why fool around with something that's already working well? I don't think it could be any better." If that's true, wonderful. Personally, I think all marriages can improve in some way. Warren Wheebe has written:

> We can benefit from change. Anyone who has really lived knows that there is no life without growth. When we stop growing we stop living and start existing. But there is no growth without change. There is no challenge without change. Life is a series of changes that create challenges, and if we are going to make it, we have to grow.[10]

Unfortunately, I see a number of couples who believe that their marriages can't be improved. This hopeless perspective makes a marriage become even more impoverished. But often this is an attitude rather than a fact of reality.

One wife who came for counseling basically wanted her husband to spend ten uninterrupted minutes a day talking with her. There was nothing wrong with this request. In fact, this is a necessity for any marriage if growth is going to occur. Two weeks later she returned for another counseling appointment, but she was quite upset. She complained because in the past two weeks they had sat down and talked only four times.

I think I shocked her with my reply. "That's outstanding,' I said. "Remember during our first session you said you were hesitant to try because you didn't think it would work?"

"Yes," she said.

"Look at it this way," I continued. "There was improvement. You're on your way to reaching your goal. If you have a 15 to 20 percent improvement this soon, you're doing well. Of course you want to have this discussion every day, but that will take time. You must have done something positive and encouraging for this to happen so quickly. What did you do?"

And all of a sudden this woman was looking at what did happen, rather than what didn't happen. It makes a big difference.

Chuck Swindoll has written:

Change—real change—takes place slowly. In first gear, not overdrive. Far too many Christians get discouraged and give up. Like ice-skating or mastering a musical instrument or learning to water-ski, certain techniques have to be discovered and developed in the daily discipline of living. Breaking habit patterns you established during the passing of years cannot occur in a few brief days.[11]

Looking Forward

When you begin thinking about your goals or vision for your marriage, there are two basics to follow: (1) Be specific and (2) look forward rather than backward. I have a phrase for this second principle—be a tomorrow person rather than a yesterday person. Usually couples want to talk more about what they don't want rather than what they do want. When you focus on what you don't want, you tend to reinforce its existence by paying attention to it. It becomes more of a complaint, and it doesn't give you any help to achieve what it is that you want. If you tell your spouse what you don't want, he or she will hear it as a complaint and will probably become defensive.

So in creating your vision for your marriage, describe what you want rather than what you don't want. Don't describe what you want "less" of, but rather "more" of, because it's easier to notice a positive response rather than a decrease in a negative.

How would you respond if your spouse said, "Have you noticed that I'm less irritable than usual?" Compare that with "I think we are getting along better and we're kinder in our responses." Begin creating your vision by stating it in terms of what will be happening. This will make reaching your goals easier than if you focus on negatives that are happening less often.[12]

Being Specific

Now back to the first basic: Your vision statements or goals need to be specific, rather than vague. Look at the following goals:

- To be more respectful;
- To improve our sex life;
- To be more loving;
- To be more flexible;
- To be less self-centered.

The first four goals are much too general. And do you see the problem with the last goal? It's backward-looking rather than forward-facing. Don't focus on reducing the negative, but on increasing the positive! And when you increase positives, the benefits are such that they begin to crowd out the negative or problem behaviors. Keep in mind that the more specific your goals, the more attainable they are. And this means they must be reasonable.

Let's look again at the goals above, and this time make them specific.

We will show more respect for each other. Each of us can show interest in one another when we first meet at the end of the day. We will give each other at least one compliment a day. We will listen to one another without interruption even when we don't agree with what the other is saying.

We will improve our sexual relationship. We will read a book on sex aloud to each other and work toward making our sexual experience creative, satisfying, and exciting most of the time. We will both communicate clearly before 8 P.M. if we are interested in sex or not. We will also be more verbal before and during lovemaking.

We will be more loving verbally and nonverbally. We will both ask how we can help the other each day. We will say "I love you" to each other at least once a day. We will make love at least once a week. We will ask what the other wants to do on Friday and Saturday nights.

We will learn to be more flexible. We will learn to handle being a spontaneous guest for dinner, and spontaneously having guests for dinner.

We will see things from the other's perspective, giving ourselves two years to accomplish this. We will do a task the way our partner does it at least once before we encourage them to do it our way. We will work toward admitting it when we're wrong and be less defensive.

These are all goals that I've heard from couples. Do you see the difference? Keep them specific, futuristic, and attainable.

Planning the Process

Goal setting and priority evaluation are not all of the process, however. Developing your plan to attain the goal is the heart of the process. Planning moves you from the present to the future.

You must be flexible and adaptable because plans do change. Locking yourself into a dead-end approach would be as detrimental to your marriage as no goal setting at all. This fact is stated in the book of Proverbs: "It is pleasant to see plans develop. That is why fools refuse to give them up even when they are wrong" (13:19, *TLB*). Planning is a tool, a means to an end. It saves time and energy, and decreases frustration.

One husband described to me how he and his wife learned to plan their goals:

> Before we were married, Evie's and my goals were just to get married. In the beginning years of our marriage, our major goals centered around my finishing seminary and getting into ministry. There were no goals for our life together as a couple except to be happy. Our first real mutual goal was to have a baby. It took us quite some time to realize that goal. Then it wasn't until we were in a seminar—a Christian Marriage Enrichment Seminar— about six years into our marriage that we thought about making mutual goals. This involved deciding upon them together and making them priorities in our lives.
>
> The experience in the seminar of setting mutual goals and then within the next few months working to reach some of those goals was so beneficial to our marriage that we decided to keep setting and reviewing goals periodically. So we began to set aside a couple of days between two and four times a year to do this. They became what we like to call "honeymoon weekends." They may not be on a weekend. We sometimes go away on a Tuesday and Wednesday or Thursday and Friday. The principle is that we get away from our regular routine and demands on our time and we go someplace where we can spend sufficient time together.
>
> We start on the first afternoon and evening by discussing goals that we previously set and evaluating the progress we've made. We also discuss setbacks and what adjustments we might need to make to reach the goals. We review the goals. About some goals we have made previously we say, "Well, that is not realistic," or "That is not practical," or "That is not so much a priority now as it was when we talked about it at the time."
>
> Then we spend some time on the second day of our honey- moon weekend talking about goals that involve others. We talk about where we would like to be in five years as a couple, as parents, as ministers, as people in our neighborhood—trying to take into account all aspects of life, including our relationship with God. Then we talk about what we would like to be doing a year from the present time in order to be on our way toward these five-year goals. We then talk about what needs to be done now to get started.

SETTING YOUR OWN GOALS

What can you do now to discover and set your goals? Ed Dayton and Ted Engstrom, in their book *Strategy for Living*, suggest six steps to setting goals. Respond to each of the following steps in the space provided.

Step 1: Understand Your Purpose

What would you like to do for your marriage, or what would you like your marriage to become? What is the general direction toward which you would like your marriage to move? Make a statement about that.

Step 2: Picture the Situation

Imagine your marriage relationship not as it is now, but as you would like it to be. What does it look like? Who are you with? What are you doing? What are the circumstances? Visualize and use your mental imagery.

Step 3: State Your Immediate Goals

What things do you have to accomplish now if you are going to move toward your ultimate purpose in your marriage?

Step 4: Act

Pick out one of the goals for your marriage and start moving toward it. Remember that every long journey begins with the first step! And before you act, pray.

Step 5: Act as If...

Act as if you have already reached your goal. If you are going to start working toward that first goal, you are going to have to start acting as if you had
really reached it. How would this impact all the other parts of your life?
What would it say about your plans for the church, your family, and others?
This may help you uncover some other goals that you need to consider.

Step 6: Keep Praying

If you are going to live life with a purpose, then you need to keep seeking
God's leading in all this. Yes, you prayed before you acted, but pray also
through the whole planning process. If you are expecting to live a life with
God's purpose in mind, you had better be communicating with Him.[13]

HOW IT WORKED FOR ONE COUPLE

Over the years I have asked couples to develop such goals or vision statements
for their marriages in the counseling office as well as in marriage seminars.

One of the best ways to capture the vision of how to develop your own
goals is to see what others have done. The following is a vision statement a
couple in their thirties developed and are now using to guide the direction of
their marriage. They said their overall goal for their life and marriage was as
follows: "Love the Lord our God with all our hearts, our souls, and our
minds" (see Matt. 22:36-40). Specifically, our goals are to demonstrate this
love to each other and others by:

Our Spiritual Well-Being
Walk together with Jesus and enjoy the journey (see Ps. 16:11).
Commit to spiritual growth through prayer, study, praise,
and meditation—as individuals, as a couple, and together with
other Christians (see Jer. 15:16).
Serve God wherever He leads us.

Our Marital Well-Being
Be encouragers by (see 1 Thess. 5:11):
Giving the other person the benefit of the doubt.
Believing in each other's dreams.
Affirming and protecting one another.
Being active listeners.
Cherishing and respecting each other.

Our Familial Well-Being
Model Christlike love (see Eph. 5:22,33).

Be accountable to God first for our family (see Gen. 18:19; 1 Sam. 3:12–14; 2 Tim. 1:5).

Uphold our home as a haven.

Our Physical Well-Being

Maintain our bodies through regular physical activity.

Our Mental Well-Being

Share interesting topics that stimulate dialogue.

Cultivate our love of books and reading.

Take advantage of continuing educational opportunities.

Our Emotional Well-Being

Recognize and acknowledge crises.

Anticipate stresses and plan accordingly.

Take advantage of available resources.

Make lifestyle changes as needed to enhance our relationship.

Our Financial Well-Being

Remember that our finances and material possessions have been entrusted to us by God (see Matt. 24:45,46).

Support our church through tithes and offerings.

Maintain a spirit of giving (see 1 Tim. 6:17–19).

Our Social Well-Being

Because we as individuals gain energy through reflection, introspection, and solitude, we must accept responsibility for our social lives by:

Developing and maintaining close and meaningful relationships.

Seeking and creating social atmospheres that are comfortable for us.

Having adequate preparation and renewal times surrounding social interactions.

Our relationship is a precious gift from God. We honor it as such, and will protect it from attack or neglect.

TOGETHER FOR OTHERS

Part of the calling of marriage is to do something together, to minister together, and to serve God together. We are called as believers to a mission to minister to others, and this means as married couples having a mission together.

One counselor stated:

> To try to keep love just for us...is to kill it slowly....We are not made just for each other; we are called to a ministry of love to everyone we meet and in all we do. In marriage, too, Jesus' words hold true: in saving our lives we lose them, and in losing our lives in love to others, we drink of life more deeply.[4]

A family therapist said:

> When families reach out beyond their own worlds to serve others, they have a stronger spiritual bond. The call to Christ is the call to serve....Every family we know that serves together regularly has a strong foundation and closeness that other families are missing.[5]

A wife said:

> Over 10 years of marriage, I have found that when my husband and I focus on our own needs, and whether they're being met, our marriage begins to self-destruct. But when we are ministering together, we experience, to the greatest extent we've known, that "the two shall become one."[6]

What is needed is *balance.* I've seen couples who focus exclusively on themselves to the exclusion of others, and those who focus exclusively on others to the exclusion of themselves.

I think one of the best mission purposes and a model for young couples today is to have a healthy marriage based upon the presence of Jesus Christ within the marriage. For years I have been dismayed by the responses of so many young couples who, when I ask if they have any models of healthy marriages, respond with, "No, we don't."

Sometimes you discover your mission as you move along in your marriage. It could be based on your experiences, or even on difficult times. In our own marriage, part of our mission to others is a ministry to couples who have disabled children, and to those who have experienced the death of a child. This focus developed because we've experienced both the raising of a disabled child as well as his death at the age of twenty-two. (See *I'll Love You Forever,* published by Focus on the Family.) From the pain we experienced and lessons we learned, we've been able to minister to others. God can do the same with the experiences of your life as well.

Well, where is your marriage going? Where do you want it to go? It's exciting to have a vision and a mission. It can make your marriage come alive in a new way, and it gives you a love that lasts!

NOTES

1. Donald Harvey, *The Drifting Marriage* (Grand Rapids: Fleming H. Revell, 1988), p. 11.
2. George Barna, *The Power of Vision* (Ventura, Calif.: Regal Books, 1992), pp. 21–22. Used by permission.
3. Ibid., pp. 28–29, adapted.
4. Phil Grand, "The Task Before Us," *European Bookseller* (May/June 1991): 48, adapted.
5. Reproduced by permission from GOLF MY WAY by Jack Nicklaus with Ken Bowden, published by Simon & Schuster, New York, NY, 1974, p. 79.
6. *Living Above the Level of Mediocrity*, Charles Swindoll, Copyright © 1987 Word, Inc., Dallas, Texas. All rights reserved, pp. 94–95.
7. Barna, *The Power of Vision*, pp. 96–98, adapted.
8. Charles Stanley, *The Source of My Strength* (Nashville: Thomas Nelson, 1994), p. 166.
9. Sheila West, *Beyond Chaos* (Colorado Springs: NavPress Publishing, 1991), p. 60.
10. Taken from a "Back to the Bible" radio broadcast.
11. Charles R. Swindoll, *Come Before Winter...and Share My Hope* (Portland, Oreg.: Multnomah Books, 1985), pp. 331–332.
12. Michelle Weiner-Davis, *Divorce Busting* (New York: Summit Books, 1992), pp. 109–110, adapted.
13. Edward R. Dayton and Ted Engstrom, *Strategy for Living* (Ventura, Calif.: Regal Books, 1976), pp. 55–56, adapted.
14. James H. Othuis, *Keeping Our Troth* (San Francisco: HarperSanFrancisco, 1986), pp. 133–139.
15. From the book *When Love Is Not Enough* by Steve Arterburn and Jim Burns and published by Focus on the Family. Copyright © 1992, Stephen Arterburn and Jim Burns, p. 6. All rights reserved. International copyright secured. Used by permission.
16. Julie Hatsell Wales, "Letters," *Marriage Partnership* (Winter 1991): 8.

–5–

WHERE IT ALL STARTED

People often ask me, "What's the cause of all the marital problems? Why can't people get along and love one another? What's the main issue?"

I have a simple answer: "The garden."

Usually that elicits a strange look, so I elaborate with five more words: "The fall of man—sin."

The world is still reaping the results of or damage from original sin—in the way we behave, the way we feel, and the way we think. And our *thoughts* are where it all begins. God pointed this out early on in Genesis: "Then the Lord saw that the wickedness of man was great on the earth, and that every intent of the thoughts of his heart was only evil continually" (6:5, *NASB*). In other versions "thoughts" is translated *imagination*. This is where it all begins—in our minds.

STORMS OF THE MIND

I've never been in a hurricane and I never want to. The tremendous force of the violent, swirling winds devastates everything in its path and leaves behind a trail of destruction. Within a hurricane there is a place called the eye of the storm. It's a place of such calm that you wouldn't even know about the fury going on elsewhere. But it's directly related to the intense violent winds as they stem outward from this core.

It's not unlike what we see in many marriages. There is an eye of the storm in every person that can make or break any marriage. It's called our thought life, and it is marred. It has a bent toward negative thinking as a carryover from the fall of mankind.

Consider these examples. A husband comes home from work early and greets his wife with a hug and kiss. But in return she becomes angry and glares at him. Why?

A wife returns her husband's overdue books to the library and he becomes annoyed at her for doing so. Why?

A husband brags about his wife's cooking to a number of friends and she becomes furious at him for doing so. Why?

In each case the spouse's positive action brought an unexpected reaction from his or her partner. The anticipated reaction would have been appreciation, not anger. What happened? Why the negative reactions? Let's go back and look at the thoughts each spouse had in response to the positive overture.

In the case of the wife whose husband came home early, she thought, *Why did he come home at this time? Is he checking up on me? If there is anything undone, he'll criticize me. I don't need that.*

The husband who has the overdue library books thought, *I was going to take those back. I'm capable of doing that. She's trying to point out that I'm not responsible. She doesn't trust me to follow through so she's going to jump in and do it herself!*

The wife who was praised for her cooking thought, *He never praises me that much at home. He's just using me to get attention for himself from his friends. He probably wants me to compliment him on something now. I wonder what they think about me now.*

In each case these reactive thoughts just popped into their minds. Has something like this ever happened to you? Probably. It could be that your thought was based on some past experience so there is a reason for it. But in each case, regardless of the intent and purpose of the partner who did something positive, the reaction was such that it might limit a positive overture the next time.

Choosing How We Respond

We can all choose to react to what our partners do with a negative interpretation, a negative assumption, suspicion over their intent, or in a guarded and defensive way. On the other hand, we could also respond at face value to what was said or done, give the benefit of the doubt, seeing it as a positive step, and showing appreciation. In the *Amplified* version, 1 Corinthians 13:7 states "Love...is ever ready to believe the best of every person."

Your negative thoughts will generate anger, but if you correct them the anger will subside.

One of the ways to keep love alive in a relationship and to keep going in a positive direction is to be fully aware of your thoughts and beliefs about your relationship.[1] If the communication in your marriage could be better, look first at your thought life. If the way you behave toward each other needs improvement, look at your thought life.

The other day I went to the dictionary and looked up the word "slander." Do you know what it means? It's the utterance in the presence of another person of a false statement or statements, damaging to a third person's character or reputation.[2] It dawned on me that many of our thoughts about one another fall into that category. God knows all of our thoughts as well as everything else. Many spouses commit slander in their minds. I've heard many such comments in my counseling office. Actually some of the thoughts we have about our partners unfortunately fall into the category of character assassination rather than character adoration. And this character assassination style of thinking generates both conflict and distance in our marriage relationships.

Couples who have growing, fulfilling marriages have thought lives that are positive and healthy. What happens within the couples is a reflection of the inner workings of each person's mind and heart.

Many, however, struggle with defeatist beliefs. I've heard many of these beliefs over the years. But as people have worked at challenging these beliefs and becoming positive, I've also seen not only people themselves change, but their spouses and marriages as well.

Perhaps it would be helpful at this point for you to take a few minutes and write out your thoughts about your marriage and your partner, so you can become more aware of whether they are thoughts that promote or hinder growth in your marriage.

1. My positive thoughts about my spouse are

———————————————————————————————
———————————————————————————————
———————————————————————————————
———————————————————————————————
———————————————————————————————

2. My negative thoughts about my spouse are

———————————————————————————————
———————————————————————————————
———————————————————————————————
———————————————————————————————
———————————————————————————————

3. Beliefs I have that help my marriage grow are

———————————————————————————————
———————————————————————————————
———————————————————————————————
———————————————————————————————
———————————————————————————————

4. Beliefs I have that keep my marriage from growing are

———————————————————————————————
———————————————————————————————
———————————————————————————————
———————————————————————————————
———————————————————————————————

ROADBLOCKS TO BELIEF

There are numerous patterns of thought that deaden and block a marriage relationship. Let me take you back to the counseling office so you can hear some of the common beliefs that impede progress.

One roadblock is *assuming*. Assumptions are usually negative. They portray the worst about another person. You make unfavorable judgments about your partner. You hear him singing in another room and you think, *He's just doing that to irritate me. He knows that bothers me.* But you don't really know that. You can't determine another person's motive.

One of the most bothersome thoughts, and a pattern of thinking that is difficult to change, is *overgeneralizing*—statements such as "He never listens to me" or "She's always late" or "You never consider what I want." What is said may be plausible to you if you're upset over a few incidents, but these words are like insecticide that drifts across a field and kills all the crops rather than just the weeds. A spouse hearing these statements usually gives up. When, in our eyes, our partners are *always* or *never*, we have condemned them and probably won't give them credit even when they please us. And overgeneralizing, again, begins in our thought lives.

There are times when for one reason or another we may *magnify*. This is the tendency to enlarge the qualities of another person, usually in a negative way. When a situation seems out of control we may tend to think this way. One husband I knew wasn't the best when it came to spending and saving money. Once, when some checks bounced, his wife shared some of her thoughts with me. "He is such a spendthrift." "He does this constantly." "We won't have enough money for the bills this month." "If we're late on the house payment again, they'll foreclose." And finally, "We're going to lose our house and it's all because of him." I think you could imagine the ensuing conversation.

Hopelessness as Blocking Belief

I've heard husbands and wives say, "Nothing can change or improve our relationship." Now that is a defeatist belief. It will not only keep you from attempting anything, but it will cause you to look at your spouse and the relationship through a negative filter. It becomes a self-fulfilling prophecy. It will keep you stuck.

Do you know what the results of this belief are? Let me give you several. And even if they don't fit you and your situation, they may fit someone you know.

With a belief such as this, you end up with a sense of resignation: "I'll just have to learn to live with this." You feel powerless and the downward spiral has started. You may begin to think less of yourself and that usually leads to thinking less of your partner. And when that happens your love and giving to your spouse begins to dry up.

I remember hearing one husband say, "I'm afraid my learning to live with it was the first step in learning to live without her." That's sad, especially since in the majority of situations change and growth are possible.

I've also talked with spouses who end up feeling like martyrs. Unfortunately, martyrs usually let their partners know what they have to live with. And in time, that hideous destroyer of marriages begins to put in an appearance—revenge. It may be hidden or blatant. All it does is cause the negatives to be set in cement.[3] (For more assistance see *How to Change Your Spouse* by Gary Oliver and H. Norman Wright, Servant Publications.)

If you or anyone else believes that nothing can improve your marriage, test this belief. Challenge it. Look at, define, and clarify some of the problems, then select one that appears to be the easiest to change. One husband wanted just to be able to have discussions with his wife without the usual defensive arguments that seemed to erupt constantly. He and I actually had an enjoyable time brainstorming different ways he could stay out of the argument and eliminate his defensiveness. We did the following:

1. He chose to believe that his wife wasn't out to get him or simply to argue with him out of spite. She might have some good ideas.

2. He committed himself not to interrupt her, not to argue or debate, and not to walk out on her.

3. He would respond to what she said by making such statements as: "Really," "That's interesting," "I hadn't considered that," "Tell me more," and "I'd like to think about that."

4. He also chose to think the following: *Even if this doesn't work the first time, I'll try it at least five times.*

5. He determined to thank her for each discussion, and when her response was even 5 percent less defensive, to compliment her for the way she responded.

Five weeks later, he called and said, "The fourth discussion was totally different. It's starting to work, Norm. You destroyed my belief that nothing can improve our relationship. There's a bit of hope now."

Perhaps it would help in countering our negative and hopeless beliefs to focus more upon passages from God's Word that are future oriented and filled with hope. For example, in Jeremiah we read, "'For I know the plans that I have for you,' declares the Lord, 'plans for welfare and not for calamity to give you a future and a hope'" (29:11, *NASB*).

Individual Action and Differences

Another defeatist belief is "My spouse won't cooperate and nothing can be done without her cooperation." Again, it's not true. We can't wait around for our partners' responses or cooperation before we take positive steps. I've had people say, "But if I do something, he may resent it or it could discourage him and make him feel bad about himself." He could, but even if he did you haven't forced him to respond in that way. And if you wait around for him to cooperate, you're just allowing his inactivity to control you. Is that what you want?

If you take the initiative, several positives are apt to occur. You won't feel so much like a victim. You'll be doing something positive, and if you initiate change or respond in a new way, your spouse may respond differently if he or she sees the possibility of something new happening. What have you got to lose? Nothing. But you do have everything to gain.

Another similar defeatist attitude is "My partner is the most entrenched, stubborn person I know. He/She is just not capable of changing." If you believe that, you will act accordingly, and he/she *won't* change, because you're not working to bring about change.

I believe everyone is capable of some change regardless of their upbringing, personality, nationality, and even age. I've heard wives say, "He's German, you know, and those men don't change." These are myths and false beliefs that we buy into and perpetuate. The reason most spouses don't change is because we believe they can't. If we respond to them in ways that don't promote change, we often cripple their attempts to change by our own unbelief!

I've also talked to couples who felt that if they tried to improve their marriages and make them better, they may become worse. But if you don't put forth the effort, you'll never know. One wife told me, "It's tolerable now. It's not what I thought marriage would be but it's better than nothing. And it's better than being alone." Unfortunately, a year later, she was alone.

If you work at discovering new information and new approaches, there's as much possibility of the relationship improving as getting worse. And frequently a relationship may get worse for awhile on the path to getting better. But it's better to be a risk taker than to be paralyzed.

Some of the other defeatist thoughts I've encountered involve personal resistance to improving the relationship. Some have said, "Why should I have to be the one to put forth all the work and effort to change?" My response is, "Why *not* you?" It would show maturity on your part and a desire for something positive. This step is a reflection of your inner character. Whether or not it has any impact on the relationship, wouldn't there be a sense of satisfaction on your part if you took this step? Not too many people think about that.

Think of it this way. Your partner may not have the same perception that you do of what is occurring in the relationship. I'm amazed at how often levels of satisfaction in a marriage can vary. One couple graphically expressed this verbally when I asked each the question, "On a scale of zero to ten, how satisfied are you with the marriage relationship?" The husband replied with a resounding, "Eight!" whereas she said, "Three." That caused some discussion.

Many times I have seen this disparity in the responses to a Marital Assessment Inventory that I have couples complete prior to coming for counseling. I ask them to complete the question "How committed are you to remaining in your relationship?" and then, "How committed do you think your spouse is to remaining in your relationship?" They respond to this on a scale of zero to ten. I don't know how many times I've seen one respond by giving an eight or nine to his perception of his partner's commitment, while in reality his partner's commitment as evidenced by her own response was only a two!

Another reason it's beneficial for you to take the initiative is because the two of you may differ in your motivation as well as in your ability to change. The person who is more optimistic or can become more optimistic, or the one experiencing the most pain, could be more motivated to take action. And both people do not have to work at the relationship with the same degree of intensity.

Libelous Labels

Watch out for "crazy spouse labels." I've heard people say, "My spouse is crazy, has a character disorder, is enmeshed with mother, an alcoholic, a pervert, sick, impossible, a stubborn _____, etc."

My response to statements like that is not usually expected. I may say, "So if your partner truly is crazy or has a character disorder, why should that stop you from working on the relationship? If the other really is that way, and we don't know that for a fact, it might even be easier to get your partner to change." They'd never thought of it like that before. It's something to consider. Throw out undocumented, undiagnosed, and unreliable labels.[4]

Victim Phrases

Not only do your thoughts about your partner affect your marriage; your thoughts about yourself will also affect your marriage because of how you limit yourself. When I work with individuals or couples I look for what I call "victim phrases."

One of these phrases is "I can't." Do you say this to yourself about yourself or your marriage? Words like these are prompted by some kind of unbelief, fear, or lack of hope Any time you say "I can't," you're saying you have no control over your life or your marriage. It takes no more effort to say "It's worth a try" or "I'll try something new," and this approach certainly has more potential. It shows you've become more of an encouragement to yourself than a defeatist.

Victim phrases that can be a real problem are "That's a problem" and "That's going to be hard." These are self-fulfilling prophecies. Also, too often we amplify them to say "My spouse is a problem" or "It's hard to work on my marriage." Whenever you see what is occurring in life as a problem or a burden, you tend to become enmeshed in fear or even helplessness. Every obstacle brings with it an opportunity to learn, grow, and become a different person if you have the right attitude. Phrases such as "That's a challenge" or "It's an opportunity to learn something new" or "Living with my spouse provides an opportunity for me to learn something new" means you're on the right track.

Another victim phrase is "I'll never be able to do anything about my life, my situation, my marriage, my spouse, etc." If you say this, it's an indication of unconditional surrender to whatever is occurring in your life. You're saying in essence, "I'm stuck in cement and won't ever be able to move." It doesn't give you or God an opportunity to work in your life. You could say, "I've never considered that before" or "I haven't tried that, but I'm willing to."

The question "Why is life...my marriage...my spouse this way?" is a fairly normal reaction to the disappointments of life, and it's certainly all right to feel this way and verbalize it. But to choose to remain at this place and stick with this attitude is crippling. I've seen some stuck there for life!

Another phrase usually follows in its wake: "Life isn't fair." That's true. It's unfair and unpredictable and it won't always be the way we want. But we can choose to grow during these difficult times and learn to ask, "What can I learn at this time and what can I do differently?"

Such victim phrases keep us prisoners in our own minds. By using them we limit growth. We limit change. We act out the rehearsal script of our minds for ourselves and others.

Sometimes thoughts like these are called "crippling thoughts" or even "hot thoughts." They lead to feelings of hopelessness, anger, resentment, bitterness, futility, and depression. What you *feel*, you will *say*—directly or indirectly—and your partner will probably respond in such a way as to confirm your worst thoughts about him or her.

Many years ago a new jail was constructed in a small town in England. The builders said it was escape proof. Harry Houdini, the great escape artist known all over the world, was invited to come and test it to see if it really was escape proof. He had once boasted that he could escape from any jail, so naturally he accepted the invitation.

He entered the cell and the jailer closed the door behind him. Houdini listened to the sound of the key being slipped into the lock. The jailer then withdrew the key and left. Houdini took out his tools and started the process of working on that cell door. But nothing happened. It wasn't working out the way he expected. In fact, nothing that he did to unlock the door seemed to work. The hours passed. He was puzzled, because he had never failed to unlock any locked door. Finally, he admitted defeat. But when, in his exhaustion, he leaned against the door, it swung open. The jailer had put the key in, but never locked it. The only place the door was locked was in his mind. Too often we're not much different.

The point I'm trying to make is this: Thoughts like these create problems. They don't solve them. Whenever you have such a thought or any negative thought for that matter, confront it. Challenge it. Debate with it. Change it. Ask yourself, "If I didn't have this thought, what's a better one I could have?" "If I could change this negative thought into something positive, what would it be?" "If someone else were to describe my partner, what would his or her description be?"

Negatives Versus Forgiveness

Negative thoughts and labeling never provide a full picture of your spouse. They are limited, biased, and slanted in one direction. More importantly, they interfere with one of the ingredients most essential for a marriage to change, progress, and move forward. It's called forgiveness. Negative labels and thoughts block forgiveness. You have to see your spouse in a new light in order for forgiveness to occur. Can you forgive a person you label as callous, selfish, controlling, insensitive, manipulative, unbending, crazy, etc.?

Labels are false absolutes. They are developed to describe those who are different. They're used to make it easier to justify ourselves and to keep us from thinking. If we used our minds constructively, we would be able to see both sides of a person. Labels limit our understanding of what is occurring in a marriage, for we see the label as the cause of the problem. Why look elsewhere!?

Labels also keep us from looking at our part in the problem. We use labels to avoid looking in the mirror for fear of what it will reflect. When you treat your spouse *as if* he or she is a certain way and possesses a particular quality, he or she may begin to act that way. Our negative expectations often become self-fulfilling prophecies and we end up cultivating what we don't want to grow.

Do you and your spouse label each other? Are the labels positive and motivating, or negative and debilitating? Are these generalizations attached to descriptions such as *always* or *never*? If you do label your spouse, perhaps you could learn to correct the label and in your heart and mind give him or her an opportunity to be different.[5]

Sometimes I wonder whether we really know what forgiveness is. Forgiveness costs. It hurts. It doesn't always come easily. Forgiveness cannot be given out of fear, but only out of love and compassion. Forgiveness is an action that lets the other person know he or she is loved "in spite of." Forgiveness is no longer allowing what has happened to poison you. Sometimes you feel as though forgiveness isn't deserved. But it never is.

That's what makes it forgiveness. It unfolds first as a decision to accept what you never thought would be acceptable. And negative thoughts and labels block that decision.

Consider these thoughts about forgiveness:

> In forgiveness, you decide to give love to someone who has betrayed your love. You call forth your compassion, your wisdom, and your desire to be accepting of that person for who he or she is. You call forth your humanness and seek reunion in love and growth above all else.
>
> Forgiveness is the changing of seasons. It provides a new context within which to nurture the relationship. The changing of the seasons allows you to let go of all that has been difficult to bear and begin again. When you forgive, you do not forget the season of cold completely, but neither do you shiver in its memory. The chill has subsided and has no more effect on the present than to remind you of how far you've come, how much you've grown, how truly you love and are loved.
>
> When forgiveness becomes a part of your life, little resentment is left. Anger may not vanish immediately, but it will wither in time. The hot core of bitterness that was embedded firmly in your being burns no more.
>
> Forgiveness comes first as a decision to act lovingly, even though you may feel justified to withhold your love.[6]

Forgiveness is a decision to wish another person well, to call upon God to bless him or her, and to show His grace to the person in a special way.

CHALLENGING THE NEGATIVE SLIDE

Here is an example of how thoughts can put a damper on an otherwise enjoyable occasion, and how to interrupt the downhill slide and move it back to the enjoyable level.

June and her husband, Frank, went to a movie and afterward Frank suggested they walk down to a restaurant and have a piece of pie. Let's look inside the mind of each as the conversation continued.

June's first thought was *Oh boy. He knows I've been trying to diet and lose weight. He's just thinking of himself as usual. You'd think he'd remember something as important as that.*

June responded with an exasperated, "No, I'd rather just go home." Frank thought, *Now what's wrong with her? We had a great time and now she's getting all bent out of shape. She sure goes up and down on her emotions.*

Frank said a bit irritably, "Fine. Just forget it."

They each walked to the car in silence, but this time something new was beginning to take place. They were both learning to recognize how their thoughts had been feeding the way they responded to each other, and so each one during their silence was working on challenging their statements or destructive thoughts.

June began to think, *Well, maybe he just didn't think about it. After all, he's not the one on a diet. I am. And he's probably hungry. I could have a cup of decaf.*

She also thought, *I guess I would prefer to go home and get some sleep. I've been overworked this month. I guess I must have snapped at him and I didn't need to. His request was innocent enough.*

At the same time Frank was thinking, *June has been pushing it at work recently. And it is 10:30. Maybe she's just tired and wants to go home.*

He also thought, *We've worked out other disagreements. I think we can work this one out.*

June, who had calmed down by this time, said, "I didn't need to snap at you. I guess I was thinking about myself a bit too much. I guess I was looking forward to some rest. And I realize, too, that you could be hungry."

Frank responded, "I appreciate your clarifying that. I know you've been working a lot. And I just remembered you're on a diet, and that eating pie in front of you might make you drool." And with that comment they both laughed and were relieved because they were learning to turn things around.

Prayer and Your Inner Dialogue

I've had counselees ask, "Is it really possible to change my thought life?" Yes! An emphatic yes, especially if you know Jesus Christ as your Lord and Savior. You won't change your inner talk or thought life by talking with your partner, but you will *by talking with God about it.* God has already communicated with us in various ways—through the gift of His Son as He speaks to us through His Word, and as we respond to Him when we pray.

When you pray, what is it like? Is it a natural experience for you? Do you use your own language and style of talking, or do you feel you must talk in a certain manner or phrasing in order to get through?

What we pray about is personal, but I would like to recommend one specific prayer: Ask God to refashion your thinking. This begins first by consecrating your imagination and thought life to God. Then ask Him to cleanse your thought life of anything that would hinder your growth and relationship with your spouse. This suggestion is in keeping with a passage of Scripture found in 1 Peter 1:13 (*KJV*), "Gird up...your mind."

The word *gird* means mental exertion. We are called upon to put out of our minds anything that would hinder the growth and development of our Christian lives—and in this case, anything that would cripple our marriages. But this growth is accomplished by the working of God in our minds. As believers, the Holy Spirit can give us greater awareness of the thoughts that control our lives and greater access to the specific thoughts that need to be changed.

With God's assistance, we can develop a much greater sensitivity to our inner dialogues. On occasion we may feel hesitant to do this because we feel guilty about an old pattern of thinking. Here again our negative inner dialogues have kept us from honest expression—with God. He will not be surprised or amazed or shocked by anything we say to Him, since He is already aware of our thoughts anyway.

As I have asked people in counseling to commit their inner dialogues to God each day, I have also asked, "How do you envision God responding to your admission of your thoughts and pattern of thinking?" This usually provokes not only an interesting response but an indication of the person's image of God.

How do we pray then? First we admit that our thought lives need renewal and changing. Next, if we lack that desire, we envision Jesus Christ as willing to help us develop the desire to change our thoughts. Sometimes you may feel justified about your thoughts about your spouse. Often people find it helpful to start the day by asking God to help them identify and dissect their thoughts and then to reassemble them. Although we may or may not be alert to these, we *can* become aware of these inner conversations. We need to develop the ability to accurately observe them. Scripture tells us to "bring into captivity every thought to the obedience of Christ" (see 2 Cor. 10:5).

I remember a counselee once who asked me, "Norm, is it all right if I use my imagination in my prayers?" He went on to say, "I find that if I at times actually imagine myself in the presence of Christ, talking to Him, it has a greater impact on my life." I told him it was fine to do so.

Some people derive more benefit out of praying with their eyes open, others by being in a room by themselves and talking out loud. Some individuals, once they have identified their negative thinking patterns, take each distorted or negative thought, repeat it, and give it over to God. Still others almost act out their prayers by seeing themselves holding each thought in their hands and literally giving it over to Jesus Christ, who accepts it with His hands and takes it away. They conclude this process of prayer by dedicating their imaginations to God in a realistic manner, especially as it pertains to their partners. Actually they have relinquished ownership of their thought lives and imaginations to God. However you do it, whatever method works for you, give your thought life to God's control.

Some people resist this approach because it is so effective! I have found it so in my own life. Some people resist giving God control because they feel comfortable with their negative patterns of thinking. They know that any effort to change would take time, energy, and patience. In fact, some gain satisfaction from their thinking patterns, even though they do not follow the direction God desires! Here is a sincere and balanced prayer I once heard:

> Lord, I am at the place of asking You to take over my thought life and my imagination. I am asking that You not only clean them up, but give me the power to control my thoughts. I am learning which thoughts cause me the most grief and which ones help me. I am learning which thoughts help or hinder my marriage. I have to admit to You that I am a creature of habit. I know I have spent years developing this type of negative thinking. I do want to communicate better with others and with myself, and I need Your help. I ask You to cause me to be very aware of what I am thinking and its effect. Please remind me, and I will respond to Your prodding. If I revert back to my old way of thinking from time to time, help me not to fall back into being negative about myself because of this lapse. Help me to be patient with myself and with You. Thank You for hearing me and accepting me. Thank You for what You will do for my thought life and inner dialogues in the future.

Some people find it helpful to conduct their own prayer sessions for the changing of their thoughts. Begin praying by affirming that the Lord is present, that you are loved by Him, and that you belong to Him. Take a pen and paper. Ask the Lord to guide your mind to thoughts you have regularly that hinder your relationships with others and with yourself. This is a private time between you and the Lord. You do not need to rush. If no thoughts come for a while, be patient. As thoughts enter your mind, write them down, but do not evaluate them. After a time, go back over the list and thank God for allowing you to remember these. Ask Him for His wisdom and guidance in changing your thoughts and in becoming aware of them at all times.

I have encouraged a number of individuals and couples to keep a daily log of their thoughts. A log or journal simply records personal insights concerning your thoughts, what you have learned about them, and how you have prayed for them. It also indicates progress in identifying, dissecting, and reconstructing your thoughts. When you write such a journal, respond to questions such as "What were the significant thoughts and feelings of this day?" and "How did I respond to them?" Write down the answers. The act of writing something down tells you that it is important.

Another variation of using a log or journal is expressing yourself in prayer. By writing out a prayer or putting it in the form of a letter to God, you give it greater thought and deliberation, and the experience can take on tremendous meaning. You may want to commit yourself to this approach for one week and at the end of that time evaluate what took place.[7]

Some couples have even done this together as a joint venture. When you are not threatened by the struggle your partner is having with his or her thoughts, you are able to offer support and encouragement. This does wonders for both your and your partner's thought life. And it gives you a love that lasts!

NOTES

1. Aaron T. Beck, *Love Is Never Enough* (New York: HarperCollins, 1988), pp. 108–110, adapted.
2. *Webster's New World Dictionary*, Third College Edition (New York: Simon & Schuster, 1994), p. 1,259.
3. Gary J. Oliver and H. Norman Wright, *How to Change Your Spouse (Without Ruining Your Marriage)* (Ann Arbor: Servant Publications, 1994), pp. 52–53, adapted.
4. Beck, *Love Is Never Enough*, pp. 155–160, adapted.
5. Paul W. Coleman, *The Forgiving Marriage* (Chicago: Contemporary Books, 1989), pp. 47–52, adapted.
6. Ibid., pp. 22–23.
7. H. Norman Wright, *How to Speak Your Spouse's Language* (Grand Rapids: Fleming H. Revell, 1986), pp. 148–151, adapted.

–6–

TRANSITIONS— FRIENDS OR FOES?

"Marriage? Sure I can tell you what it's like," said my counselee, Ellen. "It's like driving on a bumpy road in a car with no springs. Other times, it's like riding on a four-lane highway, with everyone picking up speed. And you can't be sure what lies ahead.

"It's a journey on a road that varies from being straight and smooth to winding, steep, and rough—with a few unexpected detours thrown in for good measure. And even though you thought you had packed for every possible circumstance, you soon discover you still left something out."

Ellen was a wife who had hit one of those bumpy stretches in her marriage, with no end in sight. "Over the past few years," she said, "I've experienced stress and loss in some ways I never expected. And that's thrown me. I'm a careful, organized person; I look at life realistically. And I don't just consider what is happening now, but I plan for the future. When I was eighteen, I studied and reflected on the different transitions that I would experience. But when some of them arrived, they still surprised me. Why? I wasn't able to handle them as well as I thought I would. Why not? Instead of feeling challenged by them, I felt threatened. Why?"

BENDS IN THE ROAD

Even though our day-to-day experiences can sometimes feel like drudgery, marriage is always full of twists and turns, bends in the road, U-turns, even temporary roadblocks and seeming dead ends. The journey uniquely blends acquiring and losing, receiving and giving away, holding and letting go. A loving, committed relationship helps us weather all of these moves.

From birth until death, life is a series of transitions. A transition is a bridge between two different stages of life. It is a period of moving from one state of certainty to another. But in-between there is a time of uncertainty. One stage is terminated and a new one begun. As you know, any new change carries an element of risk, insecurity, and vulnerability—even change that is predictable and expected.

Following childhood and adolescence, for most people there is the transition from being single to being married, from the twenties to the thirties, the thirties to the forties, from being a couple to being parents, from being parents to the empty nest, from the empty nest to becoming grandparents, from being employed to retirement, and so on. These transitions are all fairly predictable and can be planned for to reduce the adjustment.

Every transition carries with it seeds for growth, new insights, refinement, and understanding. But in the midst of turmoil, sometimes the positive aspects seem too far in the future to be very real. There is also a sense of loss that may or may not be recognized.

One of the natural transitions of life begins in our first year. Our baby teeth come through after bouts of pain and crying. We have gained a valuable tool for continued growth. But one day, these hard-earned baby teeth begin to loosen and wiggle. Soon they either fall out or have to be gently pulled out. We must suffer this necessary loss to make room for our permanent teeth. Sometimes we end up losing these as well, and have to be fitted with false teeth. None of these transitions is easy or painless.

DEALING WITH TRANSITIONS

Some people wish life was like a video player. Then whenever they find a particular stage especially satisfying, they can just hit the pause button and remain there awhile. But life is not a series of fixed points. Stable times are actually the exceptions; transitions are the norm. Dr. Charles Sell uses an apt analogy to describe these normal transitions in life:

> Transitions are mysterious, like an underground passageway I once saw in a tour through a castle. The castle's rooms were gigantic, the woodwork extravagant, and the huge beams in the inner part of the towers projected massive strength. But what captivated me the most was that underground tunnel. A half-mile long, the escape route led from the castle to the stables. It was strikingly different from the rest of the castle.
>
> The vast ballroom offered its visitors the feeling of dignity. A sense of comfort overtook us in the luxurious bedroom suites. Serenity filled the garden room. But the secret tunnel was mysterious and unnerving. It held no comfortable chairs because it was not a place to rest. No artwork adorned its moist, dark

stone walls. It was not a place to browse. The tunnel was not made for stopping. It was for those en route with a sense of urgency. It turned your mind to either the past or the future: either you would concentrate on the extravagant castle you were leaving behind or on the stables ahead.

Life's transitions are like that, going *from* somewhere *to* somewhere. The present circumstances may seem like a void. It would be pleasant to turn around and go back to the security left behind. But because that is impossible, it is necessary to keep groping for what is ahead; then there will surely be a resting place. Uncertainty cries out "How long?" And anxiety questions, "Will I ever get through this?"

Drawn to the past by warm memories and yearnings, the future simultaneously beckons with a mixture of hope and fear. Sometimes depression opens its dark pit. Above, the grass is green, the sun shining on gleeful men, women, and children. But those in transition feel distant from them, pressured by the urgency to get on, to get through and out. Each transition carries with it the death of the previous state and the birth of a new one.[1]

We are always moving from, into, through, and out of something or other. Resisting this process puts us at the mercy of what is happening. Which of the transitions in your life have given you the greatest sense of joy? Why? The greatest sense of loss? Why? What about your partner?

But most people do not plan adequately for transitions, and the new stages of life creep up on them unaware. Suddenly they feel carried away by a flood, totally out of control. That in itself can threaten a marriage. And to make matters a bit more tense, there can be those unexpected events that occur in the midst of predictable changes—miscarriage, marital separation and divorce, illness, disability, death of a loved one, loss of a job, relocation of the household, parents coming to live with you, an adolescent running away or using drugs, an automobile accident, fire in the home, changes in socioeconomic status, and tornadoes. The list never ends.

Sometimes we take on additional, unexpected new roles such as becoming part-time students while continuing as homemakers or full-time employees, or becoming foster parents while still parenting our own children. We may even exchange one significant role for another. You graduate from school and instead of being a full-time student, you are a full-time employee. You experience a death and must give up a loved one. What transition might you experience in the next five years? How do you think it will affect you and your marriage? What could you do to prepare for it now?

Some people seem to cope well with unexpected crises. They stay in control by taking on each situation one at a time, while delaying their response to others. Others are thrown into stressful upheaval when too many unantici- pated events happen all at once. "Oh, no! Not something else!" we cry. "This is the last straw." We can begin to crumble when our resources seem to have been exhausted.

STEPPING THROUGH TRANSITIONS

What can we do when we're in the midst of a transitional struggle? First we need to identify what is making the adjustment particularly difficult. This can affect the health of our marriages.

Identifying the Problem

The problem may be a normal change of life, or one of the unexpected events mentioned above. But most problems encountered during such a transition center on one of the following:

1. We could be having difficulty separating from the past stage. We might be uncomfortable with our new role at this time of life.

2. We could be having difficulty making a decision concerning what new path to take or what plan of action to follow in order to negotiate this new transition.

3. We could be having difficulty carrying out this new decision because of a lack of understanding of what is involved in making the change. Perhaps we lack enough information concerning expectations for ourselves and others. We could also be struggling with our own lack of preparation for this transi- tion.

4. We may already be in the midst of this transition, but we may be hav- ing difficulty weathering the period of adjustment until the new changes have stabilized. Again, we could be lacking information or resources that are needed to make the change secure.

To move effectively through a time of transition in marriage, I would rec- ommend an orderly progression of steps. First of all we need to *identify the target problem* in terms of the specific difficulty that we feel at this time and what we are willing to work on. Second, we need to *identify the target goal*, that is, the situation in which we feel we could move ahead. This goal includes specifying what it would take to feel competent in moving forward in our lives again. The third step is to *identify the tasks* that need to be accomplished in order for a smooth transition to occur. And it helps if you *work together as a couple* going through this stage of growth. If you are presently facing a tran- sition, you may want to stop and discuss this now.

Some transitions are quite normal, but nonetheless involve major changes. People marry, have children, the children go to school and then move into adolescence and adulthood. Other events can be more wrenching, affecting us in ways we never expected. We've identified some of these.

Positive events can have the same effect, such as a move, a promotion, the birth of twins, or finally having a baby after seventeen years of being without. Some adults bypass many of these natural transitions, especially if they never marry or if they die in their forties.

A sudden change can become a threat to whatever marital balance has been achieved. It tends to reawaken personal insecurities that the marriage has successfully overcome or held in check. You've noticed how sick people tend to fall back into childish ways—they become terribly dependent, demanding, and unreasonable. Similarly, some people regress in other kinds of emotional crises. Long-conquered patterns of behavior reassert themselves, at least until the first impact of the shock has been absorbed.[2]

During any major transition, people must restructure how they view their roles in life and plan how to incorporate the changes. They need to put forth a tremendous effort to give up old patterns of thinking and activity to develop new ones. Whether or not this transition becomes disastrous depends upon the person's ability to handle this process of change in a healthy way.

One of the greatest determinants of whether a transition involves excessive stress and crisis potential is the timing of such an event. Serious difficulties can occur when the accomplishment of tasks associated with a particular stage of development is disrupted or made extremely difficult. For example, an athletic husband suddenly becomes a paraplegic because of a diving accident, and must rethink his whole life.

ORDINARY PASSAGES

Predictable transitions do not have to become major storms in our lives. We don't need a satellite weather picture to tell us they are coming. Just consider your age and what stage you and your spouse are in. What is the next event looming close on your horizon? You can prepare for it and even rehearse mentally what you will do when those events occur. And you can gather new information to assist in the transition process.

A teacher who realized he would have to retire in ten years determined to expand his interests. He began to take courses at the local college in subjects he thought he might have an interest in. He took up photography and began reading in areas he had never considered before. He also began developing a list of projects he would like to tackle, health and finances permitting, upon retirement. Since there would be a significant loss in his life—his job and his livelihood—he planned in advance for a variety of replacements and worked through some of those feelings of loss.

He also had the foresight to develop hobbies that could be enjoyed whether his health was good or poor. By anticipating what was to come, he eliminated the possibility of the transition becoming a crisis. That is very important because studies indicate that many men have a serious and often unsuccessful adjustment when they retire. Depression hits many, and the suicide rate more than triples for men over the age of sixty-five!

More and more retirees seek out the so-called comfort and support of a retirement community. Jim Smoke puts a different perspective on this option:

> Retirement communities are filled with once-important people who are living out their lives in personal obscurity. While most probably enjoy their new life of leisure, many others turn to drugs and alcohol, the silent killers in scores of retirement enclaves across America, to deaden the pain caused by loss of identity and self-worth. Prescription drugs follow close behind as the killer of past dreams and present realities. As a result, in many instances retirement kills people quicker than most diseases. It happens because it takes something from them that many are not ready to give up: their identity. Mundane card games and craft classes after a daily round of golf cannot give meaning and purpose to life after one has impacted others' lives for 40 years.
>
> In most cases, retired men lose their identities quicker and more often than retired women, perhaps because many women consider themselves still "employed" as homemakers, wives, and mothers. There are abundant tales of retired husbands following their wives around all day long, looking for some form of meaning and fulfillment.[3]

Patrick Morley, in his excellent book *Two-Part Harmony*, shares this about older age:

> Once I was invited to preach the Father's Day sermon at a particular church. When I arrived I was taken aback by how few men appeared to be of fathering age.
>
> I asked the youth pastor, "What percentage of the congregation would you estimate to be elderly (over sixty-five)?"
>
> "Seventy percent," he immediately responded.
>
> "And of those, what percentage would you say are lonely?" I further inquired.
>
> "All of them."
>
> Recently a retired man told me, "The notion that when you retire your financial needs will go down is a myth. The trouble

is that you build yourself into a certain lifestyle. It's not that easy to just up and change everything."

"How much money is enough, then, to retire?" I asked.

"You can never have too much retirement income," came his reply.

There are two great problems in retirement: *loneliness* and *money*.

As a general rule, the quality of our relationships in retirement will mirror the quality of our relationships today. Loneliness is a choice, one that we make years before we retire—a decision we are making right now. True, some people won't be lonely even if they retire to the North Pole and talk to penguins all day. For most of us, though, the decisions we make right now determine whether we will be lonely in retirement.

We can avoid loneliness in retirement by sound planning and making some investments in other people's lives. The Bible proclaims that we reap what we sow.

There are two ways to be lonely: One is to be alone; the other is to have nothing in common with your mate. No married person ought ever to be lonely.[4]

These words of wisdom need to be considered decades before we get to this stage.

If moving through the various stages of life went smoothly and everything were predictable, life would be fairly easy for most mature individuals. But two factors must be considered. First, many of us are not yet mature enough nor able to take responsibility because we are stuck in our own development at an earlier stage. We may be age thirty or thirty-five chronologically, but only twenty emotionally. And second, as I mentioned earlier, some changes either come in like sudden invaders or do not occur in the time sequence that we have anticipated.

Some roles in life are not replaced by other duties, leaving a void, such as retiring from work without finding a fulfilling task in retirement, or losing a spouse without remarrying.

There are also physical changes such as the loss of one's hearing, being confined to a wheelchair for years and then regaining the ability to work, or moving from being thin to becoming obese.

CHANGES: "ON TIME" AND OTHERWISE

Transitions can be swift or gradual and may have either a positive or a devastating impact upon our lives.

Most people have heard of the phrase "male midlife crisis." But did you know that only a minority of men experience a full-blown midlife crisis—and that this crisis is not inevitable? All men do go through midlife transition, which is a normal change. But we can fairly accurately predict the man who is a candidate for a full-blown crisis. He is the person who:

- Builds his sense of identity upon his work or occupation, which becomes the source of meaning in his life;
- Is out of touch with his emotions or feelings and has not learned to accept and express them;
- Has not learned to establish close intimate friendships with other men.

Now this is a simplified evaluation, but it does hold true for most men. A man does not have to go through this crisis that in most cases creates a crisis for his family and fellow workers as well. He does have a choice.

Even if we don't stop to think about it, we all have timetables for our lives. In premarital counseling, I ask couples when they plan to become parents, graduate from school, move to a higher level of responsibility in their careers, and so on. Some of them have developed very precise timetables. Most people have their own expectations for when certain events will occur—a sort of "mental clock" that tells them whether they are "on time" or not in terms of the family life cycle.

When an event does not take place "on time" according to someone's individual expectations, a crisis may result. Many mothers face an adjustment when the youngest child leaves home. But this predictable stage can be planned for in advance. When the child does not leave home at the expected time for some reason, a crisis can often occur for both parents and child.

Having an event happen too early or too late in our plans can deprive us of the support of our peer groups. June, for example, wanted a child early in life but didn't have one until three days after her thirty-seventh birthday. Consequently, she lacked the support of many other women her age. Surrounded by women who were having their first child in their early twenties, June felt unable to develop any close friendships at this stressful time of her life. Most of her contemporaries had gone off to work.

By being off schedule, we may also feel deprived of the sense of pride and satisfaction that often accompanies such an event. Some people have worked out mental timetables for advancement in their work. But what happens if that sought-after promotion occurs two years prior to retirement rather than fifteen years earlier? We can begin to wonder: Is it really recognition for accomplishment or merely a token gesture? When an event occurs later than expected, its meaning is often lessened.

On the other hand, having an event occur too early can also limit us from preparing adequately. A young mother who is widowed early has to support her family during a time when most of her friends are married. An oldest son may suddenly have to quit college and take over the family business because of some unexpected event, even though he feels ill equipped for this new role.

My wife and I entered the "empty nest" stage approximately seven years ahead of schedule. When our daughter, Sheryl, moved out to be on her own, we should have been left with a thirteen-year-old son at home. But he was a profoundly mentally retarded child, much like an infant, and he had left home at the age of eleven to live at Salem Christian Home in Ontario, California.

We had planned for his leaving for two years by praying, talking, and making specific plans and steps to follow. Therefore, his departure and that of our daughter were fairly easy transitions. But when Sheryl told us a year and a half later that she wanted to come back home and live for a while, we faced a more difficult adjustment. We had very much enjoyed being just a couple again and hadn't expected her to return.

TRANSITIONS CONNECTED WITH AGING

When we are young, some of our losses are celebrated as much as they are mourned. Most of the early ones are developmental and necessary. We can accept these natural transitions fairly easily. But often we focus on the gain without remembering that it usually carries some loss along with it. When we face the developmental changes connected with aging, the losses affect us much more heavily because the attached gains are often lacking.

Those over forty usually experience more of the releasing and losing part of the family journey that goes hand in hand with the gathering and accumulating. R. Scott Sullender describes this later stage of life:

> The middle years of adult life are spent building. We build a family, a career, a home and place in the community. It is a time for planting roots deep into the soil of our psyches. We build memories that last a lifetime. We form deep emotional attachments with one another. The latter half of life, however, is a time when what has been built up gradually dissolves. One by one (or, sometimes, all at once) we must let go of family, career and home.[5]

Many transitions in life are related to aging. As we grow older, our childhood dreams and beliefs often begin to crumble or change. Then come the physical losses attending the usual aging process. Ironically, one change typical of middle age involves gain...those unwanted pounds and inches! We gradually lose our youth, our beauty, our smooth skin, our muscle tone, our shape, our hair, our vision and hearing, our sexual ability or interest, and so on.

In the later years, losses take on a different flavor. They seem to be more frequent, permanent, and in many cases, negative. Who rejoices over losing hair and teeth, or graduating to bifocals or even trifocals? We don't usually call these "growth experiences." Our losses seem to build on other losses.[6]

In our younger years, we may have one or two physical problems, which are often correctable. But later on, bodily ailments accumulate faster than our abilities to resolve them. Muscles don't work as well or recover as quickly. Our response time slows down. Our eyeglasses prescriptions need to be changed more often. One day we suddenly notice that people seem to be talking in softer tones. We soon have to turn up the television volume along with the thermostat!

Marriage After Midlife

Some definite changes impact marriages at this time.

Harold Myra was publisher of *Christianity Today* and was middle-aged at the time he wrote "An Ode to Marriage," a poem about marriage in the middle years. His poem illustrates the problems and potentials of midlife marriage.

"You know, it could happen to us," you said to me,
sitting in your favorite chair as we sipped coffee,
digesting the news of the latest couples splitting up.
"No matter how great we think we have it,
        if all those people can break up
        it could happen to us.
We're humans like them.
It is possible."

I didn't answer for awhile.
We were both incredulous at the news.
Men and women of maturity
        decades–long marriages
        so many have exploded, one after another.
Almost every week, another set of names.
Not him! Not her!
They're too sensible, too solid.

"You're right," I finally admit.
We've never joked about divorce,
        never brought it up as an option.

We declared total commitment to each other
          and must reaffirm that always.
But maybe realizing it could happen to us
          helps us make sure it won't.

How terrible to think of an argument
          someday when one of us feels
          the need for the ultimate weapon,
"Well, obviously there's no sense staying together.
 We're just hurting each other,
          just keeping each other trapped."
Those are words mouthed in kitchens
          and bedrooms of "mature" Christian homes.

Remember how our love began?
Years ago, I offered you my arm
          that September night we first went out.
You reached for it
          as we leaped a puddle together.
Then you walked just close enough
          to show you liked it.
I glimpsed your face under the streetlight,
          excitement splashing gently on it....
No commitment—just beginnings.

My arm pulled you that January eve
          tight beside me in that car.
Midnight. Time to leave.
"Good night" wasn't quite enough,
          and our lips touched gently
          in a kiss as light as angel cake.
"I like you," it said.
          but nothing more.

November air had rough-scrubbed our faces.
As we wrestled playfully
          in your parent's farmhouse.
That moment I knew
          and breathed into your hair,
"I LOVE YOU."
The words exploded around us.
They meant far more than "you're nice."

They meant commitment.
Your words came back to me
          in firm, sure sounds:
"I love you, too."
And our kiss of celebration
          was the beginning of a new creation.
Yes, I chose you.
Out of all the lovely girls I knew.
I chose you.
How marvelous are the women of planet Earth,
          hair flaring in the wind
          rich browns and golds
          a thousand delicious shapes
          girls who laugh saucily
          girls who read Browning
          girls who play sitars
          girls who fix carburetors.
Of all those fascinating possibilities,
I chose you.
Decisively. Permanently.
Is that self-entrapment?
Was a commitment made in youth
          to bind me a lifetime?
Ah, but it was as strong as birth,
          a fresh creation,
          soon to be a new flesh,
          you and I as one.
We chose each other.
We created something new under the sun.
You to shape me
          and I you,
          like a Luther Burbank original.
We, our own new creation,
          to produce fruit wholly unique,
UNIQUE IN THE UNIVERSE!
Then the wedding
          flying rice and honeymoon
          days and nights together.
Two persons
          as unalike as birch and cypress
          had chosen each other.
The heavens laughed

and the sands of earth
lay ready for the tender feet
of our newborn self.
Does time change all that?
Were we naive? Now, after we have
loved, argued, laughed, given birth,
what does it mean
when I hold you and say,
"I love you"?
Without the young–love ecstasy,
is it required rote
or reaffirmation of our new creation?

"I love you."
My temples don't pulse as I say it.
My body does not ache for coupling,
not as it did.
Yet the words carry more fact
than ever they did in courtship.
They embrace a million moments shared....

Standing together
atop Cadillac Mountain
and aching to absorb the blue–white–green
beauty....
Or angrily expounding to each other in the kitchen
about our particular stupidities,
then sharing a kiss ten hours later....
Bonding moments, holding us together.
How easily those bonds could be tyrannical.
"You always forget...." "You never think...."
And bitter moments bite into their flesh
with binding ropes that tie them to the
time and place instead of to each other.
Yet bonds can be a
thousand multicolored strands
of sorrow, joy, embarrassment,
of anger, laughter shared
as we watch God maturing us,
as we gently tell each other
of our joys, our fears,
even of our fantasies.

Rope is rope.
Experiences are much the same:
> crabby days
> laughing days,
> boring days.

We'll go through them "in love,"
> by commitment to each other,

sharing, forgiving,
> not blaming, not hurting.

Yet when we do hurt,
> we ask forgiveness,
> so the ropes will bind us together.

For if they don't
> they'll wrap around our throats,
> so that each struggle will tighten the noose,
> and we'll have to reach for the knife to cut the
> bonds.

"I love you."
It sounds trite—
> but not if it's remembering
> the thousands of strands
> of loving each other when we don't feel lovely,
> of holding each other,
> of winking across a room,
> of eating peanut butter sandwiches beside the surf.
> and of getting up in the morning thousands of

times, together,
> and remembering what we created
> the day we first said "I love you,"

Something permanent
> and growing
> and alive.[7]

Frequency and Finality

The nature of losses as we age is compounded by their growing frequency. We don't usually lose many of our friends through death early in life. But in our later years, such loss becomes much more frequent. The longer we live, the more friends and relatives we usually lose. Visits to the funeral parlor become almost second nature.

We seem to handle loss best when it is infrequent. But after midlife, we typically move into a time zone of accumulated losses. It can be difficult to handle the next one when we are still recovering from the present one. Our coping skills soon become overtaxed. If they were never highly developed to begin with, serious and frequent losses can hit us like a freight train.

Losses in later life often loom with growing finality. Losing a job at age twenty-seven simply means we have to look around for a new one. But losing a job of many years' duration at age fifty-seven can mean big trouble. Now what—especially if demand for our skills has significantly decreased over the years?[8]

Family Transitions

These later years carry such numerous changes—many of which are out of our control—that we need to face how we feel about what is happening to our family lives.

One of the biggest transitions your marriage faces is the time when your children leave home. Sometimes both generations look forward to this day with joyful anticipation. Greater freedom looms on the horizon for the parents as well as the child.

But once more the gain carries inherent losses. Parents must face a significant change in the amount of control they have over their kids. If the kids choose a lifestyle contrary to the way they were raised, many parents battle feelings of failure. Children may have been the mutual bond that held the husband and wife together. What might happen when that glue is no longer there? I've heard some couples say, "Yes, it's true our children are leaving and we're losing them from the home, but our gain will be our grandchildren." But what if the grandchildren are delayed for ten more years, or never arrive at all?

Having our children leave home doesn't mean just empty rooms, but emptiness in other ways as well. When our children marry, it is their choice of when and if they will have little ones of their own. Sometimes parents seriously violate boundaries by their persistent insistence that their children "get with it" and have children. We must always ask if our concern is primarily for the child, for ourselves, or for our own marriage.

Any major transition has the potential of becoming contaminated by side effects and personal feelings.[9] Having completed the major task of parenting may stimulate emotions ranging from relief to sadness over the loss. Some still attempt to live out their own lives through the lives of their children—with predictable consequences for both. For many the most painful feeling of all is no longer being needed—often a symptom of having based one's self-esteem and identity solely in the life of the offspring.

I have counseled with a number of parents who were extremely bitter when their children left. As one parent said, "I really feel left out now. They didn't turn out the way I wanted and now that they've moved 2,000 miles away, what chance do I have to influence their lives?"

Other parents become bitter because their overly indulged children ended up becoming takers, adults who didn't learn to give and respond in the same manner as their parents. Perhaps they were trained too well.[10]

Here are many of the typical thoughts parents have expressed when the time comes for their children to leave home. The range of feelings runs the gamut.

"I miss the early years with my children. I was so tied up in work at that time."

"The nest doesn't seem to empty as fast as I want. They're sure slow in moving out."

"I looked at that small chair and started to cry. It seemed like yesterday my son was sitting in it."

"I'm sure I'll be glad when they leave. But won't I feel useless?"

"That room seemed so empty when he left."

"I'm looking forward to a new job! This time for pay!"

"Now that they're gone, we sit, we don't talk, don't look at each other. Nothing!"

"Parenting is hard work and I want to get out of this job."

"We married at twenty and had the first one at twenty-two. The last one came at thirty-four. He left when he turned twenty-one. Why didn't someone tell us it would take twenty-nine years until we were alone again as a couple!"

"We're adjusted to their being gone. I hope none of them divorce or lose a job and have to move back. I like this setup!"

"I don't want to build my happiness on when they call, write, or visit. I need my own life now."

"They left too soon, married too young, and had kids too soon. I hope they realize I'm not their baby-sitter. I raised one family, but I'm not going to raise another!"

"I've done what I could. They're in the Lord's hands now. And I guess they always have been, come to think of it."[11]

When people are learning to fly a plane, an instructor is constantly by their sides in the cockpit until their first solo flight. That day is a huge event for most novice pilots, the time to launch out on their own and put into practice what they have learned. Both instructors and students can be scared. If a novice pilot is pushed to solo too soon, he or she could either crash or develop a pattern of mistakes that is difficult to change.

As parents, most of us pour ourselves into our children. They're one of our greatest investments. But unfortunately, I've seen many people build their lives around their children and end up feeling absolutely empty when they are no longer around. Life goes on, however. The normal life span of today means that we could spend two-thirds as much time in the period after child rearing as we do while going through it.[12]

MAKING POSITIVE TRANSITIONS

Where do we go from here? What can we learn from those who seem to cope better with the predictable changes of life as well as some of the sudden ones?

People who make positive transitions are people who face life and prepare in advance. They are also able to adjust and sort out which crisis needs to be handled first. For example, one man was facing the crisis of his wife being seriously ill in the hospital. Then the next day a major crisis threatened his business. Instead of attempting to juggle both and deal with them as problems of equal weight, he decided that his wife's recovery was most important and nothing else was going to deter him from helping her. Thus in his own mind the business crisis receded in importance. The second crisis did not add as much to his level of stress as you might expect. By making the decision he did, he was able to stay in control. That is important. When we feel as though we are in control, we handle life better.

If you find that you are facing or are in the midst of a transition, here are some suggestions:

1. Look at the stage of life you are leaving. Are you fighting leaving it in any way? What is there that you do not want to give up or change? What makes you uncomfortable with the new role? What would make you more comfortable? Find someone with whom you can discuss your answers to these questions.

2. If you are having difficulty making a decision regarding a new change or determining what plan to follow, seek the advice of someone you respect whose insights will help you.

3. Make a specific list of what is involved in making this change in your life. Look for the information through reading and asking others about their own experiences.

4. Spend time reading the Psalms. Many of them reflect the struggles of humanity, but give the comfort and assurance that are from God's mercies.

5. Identify specifically what you need to do at this time that will help you feel as though you have some control of the situation. And remember that being in control does not mean that you have all of the answers, or that you know the outcome or when the situation will be resolved. Being in control means that you have given yourself permission not to have all of these questions answered. You have told yourself that you can handle the uncertainty. Being in control means that you have allowed Jesus Christ to come and stand with you in this time of uncertainty. His presence gives you the stability and control you need.

Christ's strength is what you need. "My grace is sufficient for thee: for my strength is made perfect in weakness" (2 Cor. 12:9, *KJV*).

Transitions are opportunities to apply our faith. And we as believers have a greater opportunity to handle crisis than others. Hear what David Morley says about this.

> The change that is so threatening to the nonbeliever is an opportunity for the Christian to exercise his faith and to experience the process of true Christian maturity. The mature Christian is a person who can deal with change. He can accept all of the vicissitudes of life and not deny nor complain about them. He sees them all as the manifestation of God's love. If God loves me, then He is going to provide an experience that makes life richer and more in line with His will. To the Christian, "All things work together for good to them that love God..." (Romans 8:28). How often we hear that Scripture quoted. How little we see it applied to real-life experiences. What God is really saying is that we should comfort ourselves with the thought that what happens in our lives, victory or defeat, wealth or poverty, sickness or death, all are indication of God's love and His interest in the design of our lives. If He brings sickness to us, we should be joyful for the opportunity to turn to Him more completely. So often in the bloom of health, we forget to remember the God who has provided that health. When we are in a position of weakness, we are more likely to acknowledge His strength, we are more likely to ask His guidance every step of the way.[13]

TRANSITIONS AND A LOVE THAT LASTS

I've had some people come right out and tell me that having a strong marriage is impossible to attain, especially in view of life's inevitable changes. Having seen many quality marriages over the years, I can't agree. Each couple will be at different levels in how well they deal with transitions, but as long as they have in mind the goal of preparing for transitions, are working toward it, and are able to perceive progress, I would call their marriage healthy.

Not every element of the marriage relationship will always be operating to the fullest degree. We all work toward ideals for which we aim rather than targets on which we can score a bull's-eye. Perfection will never exist in this life, but that doesn't keep us from working toward the goal. Perhaps these ideas offered by David Morley can give you a new sense of vision. Remember, without a vision, a person or a marriage can perish.

In the latter part of the 1980s, a series of movies called "Back to the Future" proved to be popular. Unfortunately, many couples live the same way today. They create for themselves a limited future for their marriages by projecting the past and the present upon them.

By becoming stuck in the dilemmas that seem so endless, married couples can fail to remember that there is a future. Especially for Christians, that future is filled with hope. Too many overwhelmed men and women mentally condemn the future to be an unhappy continuation of the past. Norman Cousins once said, "We fear the worst, we expect the worst, we invite the worst."[14]

Scripture holds out a sure promise for our marriages as well as our individual lives: "'For I know the plans I have for you,' declares the Lord, 'plans to prosper you and not to harm you, plans to give you hope and a future'" (Jer. 29:11, *NIV*). When you capture the truth of these words, your marriage has a limitless future.[15]

NOTES

1. Taken from *Transitions* by Charles M. Sell. Copyright © 1985, Moody Bible Institute of Chicago. Moody Press. Used by permission, p. xi.
2. Clark Blackburn and Norman Lobsenz, *How to Stay Married* (New York: Cowles Books, 1968), p. 196.
3. Jim Smoke, *Facing 50* (Nashville: Thomas Nelson, 1994), pp. 148–149.
4. Patrick Morley, *Two-Part Harmony* (Nashville: Thomas Nelson, 1994), pp. 234–235.
5. Reprinted from *Losses in Later Life* by R. Scott Sullender, © 1989 by R. Scott Sullender. Used by permission of Paulist Press, p. 54.
6. Ibid., p. 3, adapted.
7. Harold Myra, "An Ode to Marriage," *Moody* magazine (May 1979): 60–62.
8. H. Norman Wright, *Recovering from the Losses of Life* (Grand Rapids: Fleming H. Revell, 1991), pp. 15–17.
9. Sullender, *Losses in Later Life*, pp. 54–55, adapted.
10. Ibid., p. 61, adapted.
11. Mel Roman and Patricia E. Raley, *The Indelible Family* (New York: Rawson, Wade Publishers, Inc., 1980), pp. 205–206, adapted.
12. Thomas Bradley Robb, *The Bonus Years*, Foundation for Ministry with Older Persons (Valley Forge, Penn.: The Judson Press, 1968), p. 64, adapted.
13. David C. Morley, *Halfway up the Mountain* (Grand Rapids: Fleming H. Revell, 1979), p. 26.
14. Michelle Weiner-Davis, *Divorce Busting* (New York: Summit Books, 1992), p. 45.
15. Some material in this chapter has been adapted from H. Norman Wright, *Seasons of a Marriage* (Ventura, Calif.: Regal Books, 1982); and *Family Is Still a Great Idea* (Ann Arbor: Servant Publications, 1992).

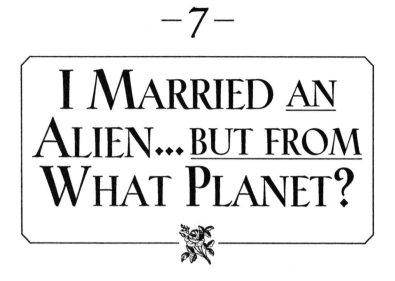

7

I MARRIED <u>AN</u> ALIEN... <u>BUT FROM</u> WHAT PLANET?

It was ten o'clock on a Wednesday morning. My first appointment was scheduled to arrive in just a minute and I looked at the names. It was a new couple whom I had never seen before. They were referred by a pastor from one of the large evangelical churches in the area. The call had come in the day before, and since I had a last minute opening, I was able to schedule them. But there had been no opportunity for them to complete the customary preliminary forms that would have given me a great deal of information. We would just have to find out the difficulties during their first session.

Herb and Sue came in and sat down, a well-dressed middle-aged couple. After a few minutes of casual conversation, I asked, "What brought you to the place of wanting to see a counselor? What are your concerns?"

Herb looked at me, leaned forward and said in a quiet, tense voice, "I want to know just one thing. I've been married to this woman for seventeen years and I can't understand why we've had seventeen years of fighting. Hassle, hassle, hassle. That's all our marriage is—*one big hassle!* We can't agree on anything. We are so different, I'm not sure we should even be married! I don't have this problem with people at work—we get along great. Now *you're* the so-called expert. You tell me why there's so much conflict in our marriage. Do other people have this many problems?"

Sue looked up and interrupted at that point to share her opinion. The next fifteen minutes seemed to escalate into a small-scale border war, and I felt I was right in the middle of it. They interrupted, raised their voices, made accusations, and threw critical barbs back and forth. Finally I raised my voice, interrupted and said, "Thank you!"

They stopped and looked at me, and then back at one another. "Thank you?" Jim said. "For what?"

"For answering your own question of a few minutes ago. You asked why you have so many conflicts. That last fifteen minutes just exposed the answers. Would you like to know what I heard?"

They both looked at me and Sue said, "Yes, I would like to hear. We've been trying to figure it out for years. What did you discover?"

I looked at both of them and said, "You asked for it, and here it is. I heard some of the most common issues that create problems for the majority of couples. I heard unresolved issues from your past, Sue, and you both have unfulfilled needs and expectations. You haven't accepted your personality differences and you are still trying to make the other person into a revised edition of yourself. You engage in some classic power struggles and you keep the conflicts alive by the intense, vicious circles you've built up. Finally, you've never learned to speak the other person's language. Now that's just for openers.

"I don't mean to be overly simplistic, but the bottom-line cause for our conflicts is our sinful natures, which leads me to another question. Where is Jesus Christ in the midst of your relationship? Have you invited Him to bring healing to the issues that are creating your conflicts? Many of these are symptoms of deeper issues."

They looked at each other silently and then back at me, nodding their heads in agreement with what I had just said. I continued:

"You're looking for a marriage of peace and harmony and one that is fulfilling. You've spent seventeen years building negative patterns. That's the bad news. The good news is *you can change*. I don't mean change your personality. The couples who make it in marriage are not carbon copies of each other. They are people who have learned to take their differences through the process of acceptance, understanding, and eventually complementation. Differing from another person is very natural and normal and can add an edge of excitement to a relationship."

A SPOUSE FROM *STAR TREK*?

Differences. How do you learn to adjust to the differences in your partner without losing who you are? How do you learn to appreciate another person's uniqueness? How can you learn to live with this person who is so, so different from you? As one wife said, "It's not just that I married someone who's a foreigner! At times I feel like I married an alien from another planet! Did I join the cast of *Star Trek* or marry someone left over from the film series *Star Wars*? Help!"

I've heard them all—questions, complaints, pleas for help. For years people have asked me the question "When you marry, do you end up marrying someone who is your opposite or someone who is similar?

My answer is, "Yes." I'm not copping out by saying that, because the answer is yes. It's both. There will be some similarities as well as opposites, and you have to learn to adjust to both. Think of it like this:

> We marry for our similarities.
> We stay together for our differences.
> Similarities satiate, differences attract.
> Differences are rarely the cause of conflict in marriage.
> The problems arise from our similarities. Differences are the occasion, similarities are the cause.
> The differences may serve as the triggering event, as the issue for debate or the beef for our hassle, but it's the similarities that create the conflict between us.
> The very same differences that initially drew us together, later press us apart and still later may draw us near again. Differences first attract, then irritate, then frustrate, then illuminate and finally may unite us. Those traits that intrigue in courtship, amuse in early marriage, begin to chafe in time and infuriate in the conflicts of middle marriage; but maturation begins to change their meaning and the uniqueness of the other person becomes prized, even in the very differences that were primary irritants.[1]

Differences abound in any marriage. Generally, they can be divided into two types. The first includes those that can't be helped, such as age, race, looks, home, and cultural background. Your personal body metabolism will affect where you want the temperature in the home, whether you wake up bright and eager, ready to face the day, or whether you need an hour to get both eyes focusing. These differences cannot be changed.

But the other type of difference involves those that can be changed. These can include personal habits in the bathroom or at the dinner table, whether you like to get up early and your spouse enjoys sleeping late, or whether one likes going out three nights a week and the other prefers watching television at home. I'm amazed at how small learned behaviors, such as having the bed covers tucked in rather than having them loose or eating a TV dinner rather than a four-course dinner on a tablecloth, become such major issues in marriage.

STAYING FLEXIBLE IN OUR STRENGTHS

We are all different. We're mixtures of various tendencies and preferences. And these are neither right nor wrong. The problem arises when one of these tendencies becomes so strong and dominant that our strengths become weaknesses. This condition fails to allow for alternate ways of responding to life. As a result, we become entrenched in our own styles and threatened by differences. Remember this: The person who has the greatest flexibility and who can respond to situations in a variety of ways will derive the most out of life and impact the greatest number of people!

What are some of these tendencies that draw us to each other but can end up being a pain in the neck? Well, some of us are thinkers and some are feelers. Some of us are savers and some are spenders. Some of us are amblers and some are scurriers. Some of us are inner people and some are outer people. Some of us are bottom-line and some are ramblers.

The factor of timing becomes an issue for many couples as they attempt to deal with marital adjustments. We all have different internal clocks within us. Some of us use a calendar to tell time, others a stopwatch. Often these two people marry each other. The wife needs ten minutes to get ready; her spouse needs an hour. The husband wolfs his food; his spouse chews each bite five times. One spouse tells a story in three minutes and the other takes ten to tell the same story.

Problem-Solving Styles

The way people approach problems and attempt to solve them can also become an issue in a marriage. Some individuals are leapers; others are lookers. Leapers do look, but it's usually back over their shoulders after a decision is made. This has often been called the intuitive approach, whereby a solution just "leaps into a person's mind." Rarely are the answers totally correct, but neither are they totally wrong. Leapers tend to rely upon past experiences to make their quick formulation of an answer to a problem.

Then we have the lookers. They are the calculators, the people who tend to do things "by the book." They look at a problem, identify the elements in it and then come up with a solution. And they often tell you that both their approach and their solution is right. And guess what. They are right most of the time! This really frustrates the leapers. But the lookers need all the available data for their decisions to be correct.

Both approaches have strengths and advantages. If you need a quick decision in an area that is not all that important, the leaper is the best one to decide. But when you have a problem that is quite important and you need all the facts, the looker is the best approach.

No couple is compatible when they marry. The challenge of marriage is to learn to become compatible. Some accomplish this within the first few years, some within ten to fifteen years, some..., well, unfortunately some never do. I know. I've seen them in my counseling office, some at seminars, some informally. But the sad part about this is that it doesn't have to be that way.

I don't care how different a husband and wife are, it's possible to learn to adjust, to adapt, to live in peace and harmony, to be compatible. I've seen it happen. One of the delights of counseling is to see couples both in premarital counseling and those who have been married for thirty years discover how to understand, accept, adjust to, and honor their partners' uniqueness.

Messages from the Trenches

I've worked with this issue for years. I've taught about it and written about it in several books. And yes, I'm going to write about it here, although in a different way. I'm going to let married individuals tell about their spouses and themselves and what they have learned. I won't give any guarantees, but I suspect that you are going to identify in some way with one or several of these people. Hopefully, you can learn from what they have learned.

These accounts are from those who have been married for awhile. Some of them struggled through this process before the pieces came together. These are people who have learned to apply and experience God's Word in their lives including these important passages:

> Let the peace of Christ rule in your hearts, to which indeed you were called in one body (Col. 3:15, *NASB*).

> Be of the same [agreeable] mind one with another; live in peace (2 Cor. 13:11, *AMP*).

Tom's Tale

"My name is Tom. I'd like to tell you about my outgoing, social wife. That's what I call her now, and that's what I called her before we married. But after about two years of marriage I started calling her 'Mouth'! She talked and talked. She even talked to herself. Now me, I'm just the opposite. I don't talk much at all. At first I was attracted to her mouth. Then I was repulsed by it. My ears get exhausted.

"I couldn't understand why Jean had to think out loud so much. It's like she wanted the whole world to know about her wild ideas. And it's not just because she's a woman. I've seen men who are the same way. But it seemed like she would start talking before she engaged her brain. At times I felt like my space was invaded by her giving a running commentary on everything or saying the same things over and over or wanting an immediate response from me on a question I'd never had a chance to think about. Man, all that stuff wore me out.

"There were even times when I'd go to the garage to putter around (and find some peace and quiet) and Jean would come out there, bring up a subject, ask my opinion, arrive at her own conclusion before I could think about it, thank me, and walk out. I'd just stand there shaking my head and wonder *Why even ask me?*

"When we go to an activity, it's like she knows everyone there and wants to stay forever. It seemed like she would never run down or get enough socializing. I've seen men like that, too. I always wondered how they did it. It drains me, but seems to give her a shot of adrenaline!

"Oh, and wait until you hear this: I think I'm a caring guy. I do give compliments. Maybe not as many as I could, but I don't think I could ever give enough to Jean. She is so capable and gifted. But it seems like she doesn't believe it unless I or someone else tell her. I used to wonder why she would come and ask me how she did or how she looked when the answer was obvious. Fantastic!

And something else that bugged me—Jean is better about this now—she would interrupt me when we talked. It takes me longer to get things out and reach a conclusion. So, if I talked or thought too slow I either got interrupted or she finished my statement for me. We had a good discussion (argument) over that one. But she's much better now, and I don't avoid discussions with her. Sometimes I remind her that our speed of thinking and speaking is different and that helps.

"When we have a conflict I think (or used to think) there was just too much talking about the problem. Jean had the belief that if we just talked it through a bit more everything could get resolved. Resolved! A few more words would be the last straw. We eventually learned to put some time limits on each segment of the conversation so I could have time to think. Then I was ready to continue. I also worked on sharing my first reaction without having to do so much thinking and editing.

"Now and then I've said to Jean, 'Honey, I want you to resolve this, but for me to continue since I'm getting worn down, why don't you write out what you're thinking or put your thoughts on the computer. Then I can read them over and be able to respond. OK?' That's worked well for us. That way Jean doesn't get as loud either, since I really tend to withdraw when that happens. I used to tell her, 'You're not going to get me to respond by shouting at me. It won't work.' Now I say, 'I want to hear you. I would appreciate it if you would say it softly and give me a chance to respond.'

"Sometimes I would ask her, 'Why are you bringing that up again? We've already talked about it.' Jean would say, 'No, we haven't.' And then we'd argue over whether we had or not. This went on for years until one day I heard her say, 'Could it be that you rehearse conversations in your mind and then think that we've already talked about it?' Bingo!—that's exactly what I do, and when she said it, I realized it. Fortunately, we've learned to laugh about it. Sometimes I catch myself and say, 'Yeah, I did talk to you about it...in my head.'

"Sometimes I worry about what Jean says to others about us and our intimacy. You know, our lovemaking. She likes to talk about it when we're not even doing it, and sometimes during a romantic time she wants to talk. That's not me. I don't say much, but I've learned that this is what Jean enjoys. And it's getting more comfortable.

"What has really helped me (and us) is to realize that there's nothing wrong with Jean the way she is. That's just her. It's the way she's wired. I guess it's the way God created her. She's OK. I'm OK. We're just different and we can learn to adjust.

"I've learned to appreciate the fact that she's helped me be more social and involved with other people. It's become apparent that Jean needs more interaction and time with people than I do. Now I'm glad to provide it. It's all right for her to go places and gab, and I can stay home or get together with one of my male friends.

"It's really helped me to understand that Jean needs to talk out loud to figure things out. And it doesn't mean that she's going to do what she's thinking out loud. She's just thinking. I've learned not to assume.

"We're not perfect, but we are much more accepting. We've learned to be creative in the ways we approach each other. And it is a lot more peaceful."

Jean's Journey
Jean shared the story of her own journey.

"Well, I'll try to be brief (that's a joke!). I'm an outgoing, talkative person who for some strange reason was drawn to a quiet, reserved, thoughtful man. I knew we were different when we were dating, but never realized just how much until we were married. When it really hit me was the evening I figured out that Tom seemed to be avoiding me. Even when I was talking to him it seemed like he couldn't wait until I quit talking. And his responses were shorter and shorter. It was as though he thought if he said less I wouldn't have so much to respond to. I guess it was true, because eventually I'd get fed up and socialize on the phone. I actually felt rejected and hurt because I wasn't getting enough talk out of Tom. I couldn't figure out why he was like that. At first I thought, *That's just the way men are.* But others I dated weren't always like that. In fact, I've known women who are like Tom. So I figured it's just the way he's wired and put together.

"I just love getting together with others. I get energized by them. But it doesn't take long (at least it seems to me) for Tom to get worn out at a party and want to leave early. I've even seen him just sit off to one side by himself or go into another room for awhile just to be alone. I used to think, *What is wrong with that man?* Then, I began to discover that Tom needs some quiet time and space to get energy back. That's draining for me, but it perks him up.

"He is friendly and communicates well, but he doesn't go out of his way to connect with people. I've got scads of friends. He's satisfied with just two. See, there's the difference—just two! That wouldn't be enough for me. I need more people to talk with. And I love interruptions. They're just great, but they really bother Tom. It's like he needs to know ahead of time that he's going to be interrupted.

"One of our biggest conflicts is, or was, in the area of communication. I like to get things resolved, and that means talking through every part of an issue. But when we talked, or when I talked, the more he seemed to retreat. So I figured I'd just keep after him and he's bound to open up. No such luck! He'd retreat, clam up, or say, 'I don't know.' I admit, I want answers right now. I used to say, 'Tom, tell me right now. You don't need time. For Pete's sake, tell me!' And then nothing. Silence. It's like I just short-circuited his thinking ability. And later on I discovered I did!

"Tom is more of what they call an inner person. Through some reading I discovered he's the kind of person who likes to think things through in the quiet privacy of his mind without pressure—and then he's got a lot to say! Little did I know this at first. Now when I need his feedback or a discussion, I just go to him and say, 'Tom, here's something I'd like you to think about. Put it on the back burner where it can simmer for awhile and when it's done, let's discuss it.' He appreciates it, and we talk more. And lest you think he always uses a Crockpot to cook, he doesn't. Sometimes it's a microwave! After I did this for awhile, he said to me, 'Thanks for recognizing and respecting my need to think things through in the privacy of my mind.' That felt good, because I like compliments.

"I've had to learn he isn't comfortable thinking and talking fast out loud. That's my world, not his. A few times we got into a conflict and I pressured him so much he just let fly with an outburst that seemed extreme. I learned not to push. It's better to let him think first.

"I've also learned to not interrupt Tom with every thought that pops into my head. I'm finally learning to edit and pick times when I can have his attention. I know my thinking out loud used to bother him, because he thought I meant every word of it. I just like to sort things out, and I don't care who knows it. So now I just warn him, 'Tom, I'm just thinking out loud again. You can relax, because I'm not going to rearrange all the furniture in the house today.'

"You know, I used to think that Tom's quietness and withdrawal at times was a passive-aggressive way of getting back at me. But it wasn't. God made me unique and made Tom the way he is. I just didn't understand it. Twice this last month he actually did some thinking out loud with me, which was wonderful. I know it was difficult for Tom, but it was great to see him put forth that effort. I hate to admit it, I really do, but now I see some value in being alone and quiet, too...sometimes...just a bit.

"I've also learned that when I encourage him to be who he is, I receive more of what I need, too. The other day I knew he was frazzled, but I wanted to talk. Usually, I would have forced the discussion or tried to, but I remembered a couple of passages from Proverbs, 'Don't talk so much. You keep putting your foot in your mouth. Be sensible and turn off the flow!' (10:19, *TLB*). And, 'Self-control means controlling the tongue! A quick retort can ruin everything' (13:3, *TLB*).

"So I said, 'You look like you need some recouping time. Why don't you go read or do whatever and maybe we could talk a bit later.' And we did talk—quite a bit. And I am learning to write him notes, too.

"Tom understands things that used to really get me. He's better at it, but I've learned that a few of his words mean a hundred of mind. When he gets a big smile on his face and doesn't say much, I say, 'It looks like that smile is about 500 of my words.' And he says, 'You've got that right. I just love good translators!'

"So I've learned to give him time and space, and not to interrupt when he talks. And I don't assume anymore that he doesn't have opinions or want to talk. He's selective and more methodical. I use a scatter-gun approach."

Sheri's Story

Let's consider another couple—Sheri and Fred, who have been married for twenty-two years. Sheri says:

"After I married Fred, the relationship was just okay. At times I felt pinned down or restricted by him. It's like he was so mechanical and precise he'd take the fun out of everything. It's as though we'd both look at the world and even though we stood in the same place, we saw something different.

"Fred seemed to have a clipboard, and was making a list of the facts. It's one thing to be literal, but at least from where I was coming from he was extreme. I know I'm not always the most practical, but Fred is overly so...and realistic...at least that's the way he sees himself. I love possibilities and speculation, but he didn't seem to see the value of it.

"We had so many arguments over (he says) my answers. I mean, he'd ask, 'What time will you be getting home?' and I'd say, 'Around five o'clock.' That wouldn't do it for him. He needed to know the exact time. If I bought something, it wasn't enough that I'd tell him it was around forty dollars. He wanted to know it to the penny.

"For several years he wouldn't ask me for directions anywhere. I mean anywhere. Even inside a building. Fred wants a detailed, step-by-step map. I can find where I'm going with instructions like, 'It's a couple of blocks or signals down seventeenth and you'll pass some kind of a school on the left, then in a little while you'll turn right and the store is, uh, let's see, two or three blocks on the right. Oh, you can't miss it.' That's not good enough for Fred. He says it's not precise enough.

"The future intrigues me much more than what's going on at the present time. There are all sorts of surprises waiting to be discovered. Fred looks at things and wants to know if it will work or won't work. I'd rather think of the possibilities.

"Whenever we buy something that needs to be put together, Fred can't wait to get into the box and find the instructions. He loves to follow them exactly. A friend of mine asked me to think of a word that would describe Fred. The first word that came to mind was predictable. I could set the clock by him. I can tell you what time he gets up, leaves the house, and what he has for lunch. He'll drive the same streets to work or church, even though we've got several options.

"You can imagine what our communication was like. I don't have the same problem with some of my other friends. But at least I always know the subject we're talking about when Fred brings it up—he identifies it very precisely.

"Actually our relationship is much better. One day we had this big argument—I mean BIG. We both got upset and said the same thing. It's funny now that I think about it, but we each said, 'There's nothing wrong with the way I see things. It makes sense to me. If you'd just try my way for a change then you'd see. And you'd understand me better. We're not wrong, just different.'

"Then I said, 'Our statement has some real possibilities. Let's look at it.' And Fred started laughing at what I said. So did I. But then he went on. 'What if, using your idea of a possibility, just what if each of us became a little bit more like the other when we're talking and working together.' When he used the word possibility, I knew it could work.

"So we're both responding differently. You know what I'm doing? First of all, I'm saying to myself it's all right for Fred to be practical, pragmatic, and literal, following instructions to the letter of the law, liking routines, and never seeing the big picture. He's got me to help him experience another way to live life. When we interact, talk, play, work, or whatever, I ask myself, 'How would Fred see this? How would he describe it? How would he respond?' For me, it's become an adventure to package my responses in a way that fits him. It's fun and I can speculate about it at the same time.

'So when I talk to Fred, I've learned (as much as possible for me) to give him some specifics or the bottom line first. Then he seems to be better able to listen to me. It's like I have to give him one point and then I can lead him to the next and the next and the next. Personally, I'd rather throw out the whole bale of hay any which way and then sift through it! But, you know, when I present something in his format, I'm able to see the pros and cons of it clearer, too. So I guess there is a benefit.

"It also helps when I ask him to listen to my wild dreams and ideas even though (and this is the important part) we may never ever do this. Once I even said, 'And before you tell me the reasons this wouldn't be practical, let me share them with you.' Boy, Fred never said a word, but he sure looked at me with all kinds of respect. Then he's willing to listen to my suggestions of why it might work.

"I used to think Fred's lack of enthusiasm for my dreams was, well, something personal, like he didn't care for me. But I discovered he's just more cautious and factual. I wished he would dream with me more, and he's doing better. He's helped me enjoy what is going on at the present. And there really is a lot happening right now. This helps him, because often he felt I didn't appreciate what he was doing right then—it seemed like I always wanted more. When I listen to his routine stuff, then he listens to me. I guess I need his practicality."

Practical Fred

"I'm Fred. Someone asked me what attracted me to Sheri. Excitement. My life was fairly routine. She brought a lot of fun and excitement into my life. But after we married, it seemed to get old in a hurry. She seemed scattered and going in several directions at once. She was always looking for some new possibility.

"When we plan a vacation, it really doesn't start for me until we get there. But for Sheri, it seems to start as soon as we mention it! She goes wild with all sorts of ideas and there it is again—possibilities of this and that. She loves the unknown. And even after it's over it seems like she's doing the same thing! I mean, when she describes what we did and where we went her perceptions are so different from mine that I wonder if we were on the same vacation. The word *exactness* isn't in her vocabulary. I ask her for something and I hear 'It's over there somewhere.'

"When I ask a simple question, all I ask for is a simple, clear, concise answer, not a hundred speculative possibilities. But she is doing better. And I've also learned that even if she gives me four or five sentences of background details, when she does give me the exact answers then I've got a very complete picture. She just takes longer and puts it in a different order. That used to drive me up a wall. Now I relax and realize it will just take a little longer, but she'll get to the point. And sometimes by hearing all that other stuff first, I listen to it better and learn about some things that are helpful. I've even said, 'Honey, here's an idea. Speculate on it for a while and then give me some alternatives.' She loves it.

"She says I nitpick, but I think she takes an incident and blows it way out of proportion. It's amazed me for years how she and the women friends who are just like her can carry on a conversation. They start a sentence and never finish it, but jump to another one and don't finish that before jumping to the next and the next. And yet, they seem to understand each other. I've tried. I mean I've tried, but it's beyond me. I've learned to say, 'Sheri, I want to hear what you have to say, and it helps me if you could condense it and finish a sentence before going on. I'll stick with you better.' And it's worked.

"I've learned that Sheri's mind and body might be two different places. We could be watching a movie together and I'm really into it, but I'll ask her a question and she's thinking about something else. I've just accepted that as part of our differences.

"I have learned that we approach projects differently. Years ago her lack of looking at the directions and following her hunches instead drove me up the wall. Now I do one of two things, because figuring things out on her own is like a game to her. I either just wait and eventually she'll ask for some help, or I say, 'Do you want me to read the directions first and go over it step by step, or do you want to wing it?' This seems to help.

"We have different definitions for words such as *No, Later, Sometime,* and *I'll get it done.* I usually ask, 'Can we clarify that?' or 'Whose definition are we using?' That's cleared up a lot of misunderstanding.

"After years of frustration, we've both learned to adjust some. Sheri has broadened my horizons. Because of her, I've followed her lead sometimes and had some great experiences. I've learned that her (what I call) restlessness is just her, and I haven't caused it. She's just a person of vision more than I am. And we've been able to discuss that it's important to me to have her notice my present efforts and contributions. I used to think she was just unappreciative, but that's not the case. She's just looking forward, that's all.

"It's best, too, when I bring something up to give her an overall general view rather than a bunch of little details. She likes it when I ask her questions, and listen. What used to be a problem for us isn't now We are learning to accept that we're different and...we need each other's differentness to make us complete. I wish we had started out our marriage on that note."[2]

GROWING THROUGH DIFFERENCES

These two couples as well as so many others have gone through the typical stages of adjusting to conflict. You're vaguely aware of them when you marry. You certainly wouldn't say at that time that your partner is different—more likely "unique." But after a while it is...different. At first you may try to *accommodate.* You tolerate, overlook, or deny differences to avoid conflict.

Then you *eliminate,* or try to purge the differences in one another by demanding, pressuring, or manipulating.

But then you *appreciate,* because you discover the differences are necessary and indispensable. They're essential.

And because of this you are able to *celebrate* them. You delight in them. You welcome them. You encourage their growth.[3]

Couples discover through this process that they didn't marry the wrong person. Think about this:

In reality, we marry the right person—far more right than we can know. In a mysterious, intuitive, perhaps instinctive fashion we are drawn by both similarities and differences, by needs and anxieties, by dreams and fears to choose our complement, our reflection in another.

We always marry the right person, and the discovery of that rightness moves us into the third marriage within a marriage. We at last begin to appreciate what we had sought to eliminate.

As we discover that we knew more than we knew when we chose whom we chose, appreciation begins to break into a gentle flame. In appreciation, we discover that people who marry each other reflect each other. There is a similar level of maturity, a parallel set of self-understandings and self-acceptance in most couples choosing each other. The two express their self-image and self-valuation in the person selected.

People who marry each other complete each other in a puzzling yet pronounced way. The missing is supplied, the imbalanced is brought into equilibrium, the dormant is enriched by what is dominant in the other.[4]

Well, what do you do now? Study your partner. Study yourself. Decide how you could respond differently. Expand your knowledge of gender differences, personality differences, and how to speak in a language that your partner understands. We've just scratched the surface here. If you want to learn more, read chapters 4-9 of *How to Change Your Spouse* (Servant Publications) and *What Your Mother Couldn't Tell You and Your Father Didn't Know* by John Gray (HarperCollins).

You may be surprised and amazed by what you discover. And you know what? It will be worth the minimal amount of time it will take to bring a new and better level of harmony and adjustment to your marriage. It's an ingredient for a lasting marriage. It will help you celebrate your differences.

The adventure of marriage is discovering who your partner really is. The excitement is in finding out who your partner will become.

Notes

1. David Augsburger, *Sustaining Love* (Ventura, Calif.: Regal Books, 1988), p. 40.
2. Concepts adapted from Otto Kroeger and Janet M. Thuesen, *Type Talk* (New York: Delacorte Press, 1988) and *Sixteen Ways to Love Your Lover* (New

York: Delacorte Press, 1994); and David L. Luecks, *Prescription for Marriage* (Columbia, Md.: The Relationship Institute, 1989).

3. Augsburger, *Sustaining Love*, p. 38, adapted.

4. Ibid., pp. 54, 56.

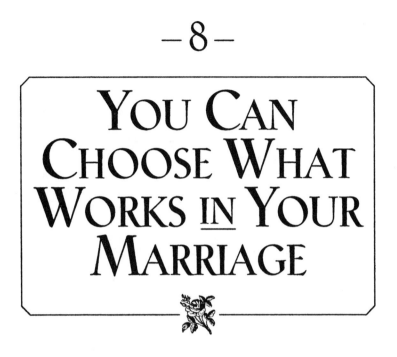

8

YOU CAN CHOOSE WHAT WORKS IN YOUR MARRIAGE

Years ago a couple came to see me with a particular problem. As we talked about what was occurring that brought them in, I discovered that this issue seemed to occur about every three to four years. I assumed that each time it happened they sought out a counselor, but that wasn't the case. This was the first time they had sought professional help.

I asked them, "Is this a continual issue in your marriage, or did you resolve it each time it happened?"

They said, "Oh, we were able to resolve it all the other times. But this time we thought we'd get some outside help."

I replied with, "Well, I'm not sure you need me. If you were able to resolve it before, why don't you just do what you did before? It sounds to me like it worked. If it was effective, why not do it again?"

They looked at me with an expression of, "Now, why didn't we think of that and save the money we're spending today?" Often this is the case. Look to see how you worked through issues before and do it again. If it worked once, it can work again. It can even be refined so it will work better the next time.

But you have to make up your mind to choose to find what worked.

CHOOSING THE SWEET LIFE

Life is full of choices. Some are difficult; others are easy. But everything goes back to a choice. We can choose to love or not love. We can choose to be committed or not to be committed. We can choose to look for the best or for the worst.

If you have ever read about or observed various animals, you may have discerned the difference between the habits of buzzards and bees. Buzzards search for food by flying overhead and looking for dead animals. When they find the decaying animal, they move in to gorge. And the riper the better. This is what they want. They have made their choice.

Honeybees, however, have different habits. They search for nectar that is sweet. They are very discriminating as they fly through the various flowers in a garden. Some flowers just don't contain what the bees want, so they move on. They make a choice about where they settle in and feast. Both the bees and the buzzards find what they are seeking. They make choices.

Couples make choices, too. And I've seen couples who remind me of both the buzzards and the bees.

WHAT IS WORKING IN YOUR MARRIAGE?

The suggestions I'm going to give you in this chapter may already have been said in one way or another in earlier chapters. But they need to be expressed again in this fashion. Why? It's simple. Because they work. I have seen them work in the lives of couples. These ideas are not original. I draw from anywhere I can to discover what works, so it can be passed along to help others.

If I were to meet you and talk with you about your marriage, I would ask you one question: "What's working?" A simple question, yet significant. I would want to know what works in your marriage. If I held a marriage seminar with 100 couples and asked everyone the question "What are the problems and difficulties in your marriage?" What do you think would be the outcome after everyone shared? There would be a dark cloud of doom and despair. Everyone would probably leave discouraged and with a lack of hope. I doubt if many would have benefited from their time together. I'm not suggesting that we overlook or ignore the problems. But there are better ways to solve them.

If I were to ask every couple to share "What is working for you?" what a different atmosphere and outcome we would have following the meeting. Couples would have been encouraged and challenged by what they heard. They would have discovered new ways of revitalizing their own marriages.

Let me turn to sports for a minute. I enjoy baseball. Sometimes even the best of the hitters face a drought. They fall into what we call a hitting slump. And they try and try to break out of it. They consult with their hitting coach and analyze what they're doing wrong so they can get back on track. Many will get videos of themselves while batting to see what they can learn. The videos they select will make the difference. Some will look at videos when they're in a slump and watch their worst performances. They think if they focus on this they can learn what they're doing wrong and correct it. Unfortunately, this doesn't work very well.

Others select older videos that show them in a hitting streak and doing fantastic. They watch and observe what they were doing that worked. Soon they're able to get back to that level. They concentrated on what was working.

Marriage isn't all that different. The best step any couple can take is to focus on what is working. This is the best way to solve problems. I'm sure there are many times when you and your spouse get along. Can you describe specifically what you and your spouse do differently when you do get along? Think about it. Identify it.

EXCEPTIONAL TIMES

I've heard many couples in counseling say, "We don't communicate." Often I ask about the times when they do communicate. I'm asking for the exceptions. Sometimes I have to be persistent and keep asking, especially when couples are full of pain and despair. At times the progress is slow, but soon I hear an exception to "We don't communicate."

One husband said, "Last Sunday after church we went out to lunch, just the two of us and we talked all right. It wasn't bad." They were able to come up not only with this exception but several others. And what happened is that these exceptions began to counter the absolute belief that "We can't communicate." This is the beginning step to building a sense of hope and optimism. The exceptions begin to diminish the problems.

Too often the longer a couple is married the more they see their partner as incapable of changing. This can be in the realm of habits, behavior, or even attitudes. But as you talk about exceptions you discover that under certain conditions and circumstances your partner is different. As one wife shared, "I used to believe that Jim wasn't interested in sharing his feelings with me. But when we go away on a trip for a few days, and especially when we get away from that darn phone, he seems to relax and get his mind off of work. Those are the times when he does open up. I wish that somehow we could create those conditions more frequently." And in time they did. She discovered that some changes were possible given the right setting.

Road Maps and Windows

Another benefit of bringing out exceptions is that they might provide a road map showing the direction to take to increase the positives in their marriage. Discovering an exception might be the window a person or couple needs to try a new path that will improve their relationship. It may help them develop a plan. So much of what happens in counseling is plan making. This was drilled into me by a man I studied under in the late '60s—Dr. William Glasser. And I've never forgotten that principle. But the plan must be your own and individualized for your relationship.

Jim and Renee were a middle-aged couple with a marriage that had stagnated. Fortunately, they realized this and one day they each stayed home from work. They went to a small restaurant that was out of the way and quiet. They told the waitress they needed a booth for several hours and would be eating both breakfast and lunch. They also promised a healthy tip. When asked why they did this, Jim said, "We wanted to get out of the house into a neutral area and the restaurant was cheaper than a hotel room. And being in public might keep us from getting overly upset."

They both talked about how they wanted their marriage to be different twelve months from then. After they agreed on what they wanted, they identified three to five steps that both would take in order to reach their goal. They agreed to take one evening each month (on the fifteenth) to go out to dinner to measure progress and refine their plan. It worked, and it was much more economical than going to seek assistance from a marriage counselor.

A final benefit of looking at an exception is that it might enable you to discover a strength. In turn, this will strengthen the relationship. It's a step of encouragement because it lets a couple know they've been doing something right after all. Perhaps this is an example of what Paul was talking about when he said:

> Whatever is true, whatever is worthy of reverence and is honorable and seemly, whatever is just, whatever is pure, whatever is lovely and lovable, whatever is kind and winsome and gracious, if there is any virtue and excellence, if there is anything worthy of praise, think on and weigh and take account of these things [fix your minds on them] (Phil. 4:8, *AMP*).

CHOOSING HOPE OVER FUTILITY

We as Christians are called to be people of hope rather than despair. We are called to be people who confront obstacles and find a way to overcome them rather than to resign ourselves to a sense of futility.

It's strange, but I've found that some people don't really want to discover the exceptions to the problem. Perhaps they don't want to hope, for fear they'll be disappointed. Some see the exceptions as just that—a rare exception that just happened. But we also struggle with selective remembering, and the painful experiences tend to lock in and persist. We emphasize failures instead of successes.

But it doesn't have to be this way. We can choose another direction. Let's consider the suggestions that numerous marriage counselors have offered to assist couples in having fulfilling relationships.

What Worked Back Then?

I've never worked with any couple that doesn't get along some of the time. We all get along well part of the time, and I realize for some it might be just 20 percent of the time. That's all right. It's enough. In order to have a lasting marriage, the first step to take is to discover what each of you are doing during the times you do get along. You can do this by yourself or with your partner. Brainstorm and figure out what each was doing before and during that time. Be sure to concentrate more on what *you* were doing than on what your partner was doing. This is the beginning point for any change. What were you thinking and feeling when you were getting along? Then plan to do more of it...regardless of what your partner does.

Sometimes people have mental blocks against identifying current expectations. If this is your problem, think back to a time when your marriage had some satisfying times in it. Often I will have couples plot out charts of the history of the satisfaction level of their marriages. They're asked to identify the best experiences they've had since their marriages. "Best experiences" may have been times of just getting along. For some that's positive! And as we discuss these in detail, we talk about how we could create some of the same experiences right now in their marriages. Here is an example of the chart, and one husband's evaluation. The * indicates his level of satisfaction.

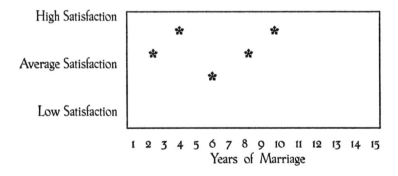

Here is the husband's analysis of his chart:

Best Experiences
　　Two years—I felt loved and accepted by you. You had an interest in me and my work.
　　Three years—I think you needed me to help with Jimmy, and that was a good experience.

Six years—Seemed to communicate real well without fighting for a few weeks.

Eight years—Started praying together twice a week.

Nine years—Had a week's vacation with no kids or in-laws; talked a lot and made love every day.

This is a good way to discover what worked in the past, to recall what we learned from it, and to put it into practice now.

Perhaps all of us as couples need to ask ourselves the question "During the positive times in our marriage, what did we enjoy doing that we haven't been doing?" Then do it. Positive behaviors and responses create positive feelings. Biblically we are called upon to behave in specific ways—and nowhere does it ever say to wait until you feel like doing it.

COMMUNICATING CARING BEHAVIORS

Over the years I have used a pattern for increasing positive behaviors for couples in both counseling and in seminars. I've talked about it and written about it before. It goes by various names such as "caring behaviors" or "cherishing behaviors." Let me present it in a way that you can do it yourself.

Ask each other the question "What would you like me to do for you to show how much I care for you?" The answer must be positive, specific, and something that can be performed daily. The purpose of each action must be to increase positive behavior, not to decrease negative behavior.

"Please greet me with a hug and a kiss" is positive.

"Don't ignore me so much" is negative.

"Please line the children's bikes along the back wall of the garage when you come home" is more specific and thus better than "Please train the children to keep their bikes in the proper place."

Ted would like Sue "to sit next to him on the sofa when they listen to the news after dinner." This is positive and specific. It's better than asking her to "stop being too preoccupied and distant" (a negative and overly general request).

Sue would like Jeff "to kiss her good-bye when they part in the morning." This is positive and specific, which is different from "stop being so distant and cold" (a negative and overly general request).

Avoid making vague comments by writing down beforehand your answers to the question "What would you like me to do for you to show how much I care for you?"

The small, cherishing behaviors *must not concern past conflicts.* Your requests must not be old demands. That is, the requests must not concern any subject over which you have quarreled.

The behaviors must be those that can be done on an everyday basis.

The behaviors must be minor ones—those that can be done easily.

These requests should, as much as possible, be something only your partner can fulfill. If they are things that a hired hand could perform, they may create problems. For example, if they are mostly task-oriented like "wash the car," "take out the trash," "clean out the camper," "have the dishes and house all cleaned up by the time I get home," etc., they do not reflect intimacy and the cultivation of a personal relationship. Some better responses would be, "Ask me what excites me about my new job," or "Turn out the lights and let's sit holding hands without talking," or "Rub my back for five minutes."

Each list should include fifteen to eighteen items. Listing as many as eighteen creates more interest and makes it easier to follow through with requests. When you give your list to each other, the only discussion you may carry on about the list is to ask for clarification if it is needed.

Now it will be your commitment to do at least two items each day on your spouse's caring list, whether or not he or she is doing any positive behaviors on your list.

Here are some suggestions for your "caring" list:

1. Say "hello" to me and kiss me in the morning when we wake up.
2. Say "good-night" to me.
3. Sometimes bring me home a pretty flower or leaf.
4. Call me during the day and ask "How's it going?"
5. Put a candle on the dinner table and turn off the light.
6. Hold me when we're watching TV.
7. Leave me a surprise note.
8. Take a shower or bath with me when the kids are gone.
9. Kiss or touch me when you leave for work.
10. Tell me about your best experience during the day.
11. Hold my hand in public.
12. Tell me I'm nice to be around.
13. Praise me in front of the kids.
14. Ask me how you can pray for me.

Many of the cherishing behaviors you request of your spouse may seem unimportant or even trivial. Some may be a bit embarrassing because they may seem artificial at first. That's all right. These small behaviors set the tone of the relationship. They are the primary building blocks for a fulfilling marriage. They establish an environment of positive expectations and change negative mind-sets.

When the lists are completed, exchange them with each other.

Discuss the cherishing behaviors you have requested of each other. Don't be hesitant about telling your spouse how you would like to have the cherishing behaviors done for you.

For example: "Ted, remember the way you used to bring me a flower when we were first married? You presented it to me when you met me at the door—after you had kissed me. It made me feel really loved."

During the discussion it is likely that both of you will think of a few more cherishing behaviors that you would enjoy receiving. Add them to the lists. The more the better, providing the lists are approximately equal in length.

The basic principle behind this approach is this: If couples will increase their positive actions toward each other, they will eventually crowd out and eliminate the negative. The consequences of behaving in a positive way override the negative. In addition, behaving in a loving, caring way will generate the habit of responding more positively, and can build feelings of love.

HOW MUCH IS IN THE BANK?

Perhaps the following concept will illustrate the process in a different way. One of the metaphors used to describe a couple's interaction is that of a bank account. There are variations of this, but one is called a Relationship Bank Account.

As is true of any bank account, the balance in the Relational Bank is in flux because of deposits and withdrawals. Relationship deposits vary in size just like our monetary deposits. They could be a kind word or action or a very large gift of love. Withdrawals also vary. A minor disagreement could be small, but a major offense could drain the account. Zingers are definitely a withdrawal, and so is defensiveness.

When you begin thinking of your relationship in this way, you can be more aware of deposits and attempted deposits as well as what constitutes a withdrawal. Naturally the larger the balance, the healthier the relationship. And just like a monetary account, it's best to have sufficient reserves in your Relational Bank Account. Unfortunately, many couples live with their balances at a debit level.

There are two types of currencies in relational accounts—his and hers. Each may have a different valuation and could fluctuate from day to day. There is a difference in this type of bank—it's the "teller" or receiving person who sets the value of a deposit or withdrawal.

If there is a large balance in the account, a few small withdrawals don't impact the account that much. But if the balance is relatively small or hovers around zero, a small withdrawal is definitely felt. The ideal is to keep the deposits high and the withdrawals low. And each partner needs to be enlightened by the other as to what he or she perceives as a deposit or a withdrawal. What is a deposit for you? For your spouse? What is a withdrawal for you? For your spouse? It may help you to discuss this concept for clarification.[1]

Sometimes I find couples might want changes that are reasonable but unattainable at first. But over the long haul they can be accomplished. Trying for the unattainable breeds discouragement. It's better to work on very small attainable goals in order to eventually achieve the possible. Achieving a number of these small steps may in time resolve the major problem. It's better to spend time working on something you can achieve than something you can't.

BREAKING VICIOUS CYCLES

A different example of this is found in an approach that some marriage counselors use to help couples break free of the vicious cycle of reinforcing undesirable behaviors on the parts of their partners. There is a way to break a pattern on your own. It's not a matter of ignoring the behaviors, but making sure you're not helping to promote it anymore. It involves doing basically what a marriage counselor would have you do if you were in his or her office. But it does take cooperation from both the husband and the wife.

The first step is to agree not to become defensive at whatever is written or said. The second is for each one to write out three problem behaviors each would like changed in their spouse. They should be listed one to three to indicate the level of importance.

The third step is to list your own reactions to each behavior to identify how you might be reinforcing this behavior. This is a very important part of the solution. The final step is to list desirable or positive behaviors you would like from your partner. Here is one wife's list:

I. Problem Behaviors of Spouse I'd Like Changed
   A. I dislike his constant complaining. He complains about everything.
   B. I dislike the way he forces his ideas, wants, and desires on me. He tries to mold me and shape me to conform to his expectations.
   C. I dislike the way he never compliments me without qualifications.

II. My Reaction to These Behaviors
   A. I tell him that that's the way it is and he can't do anything about it. Often, I say nothing and just keep it inside.
   B. I am usually hurt by this and get angry and try to say something that will hurt him in return. I also tell him that I'm sorry that I'm not what he wants me to be.
   C. I respond by usually saying nothing—just keeping it inside. Just some kind of recognition would really help.

III. Desirable or Positive Behaviors of Spouse
   A. It's nice when he gets excited about something we can both do.
   B. I like it when he compliments me in front of other people.
   C. I appreciate his doing the dishes.

This is a list from her husband:

I. Problem Behaviors of Spouse I'd Like Changed
A. She has no desire for sex. She laughs when kissed—shows no sexual interest at all.
B. She walks away from me when I am talking to her. She usually tells me to shut up.
C. She spends the little time we have together picking up things, taking showers, doing odd jobs, etc.
II. My Reaction to These Undesirable Behaviors
A. My first reaction was to kiss her. When I found out that this turned her off I stopped, trying not to push what obviously annoyed her.
B. I usually get mad and say things again to make sure she understands.
C. I usually sit there although sometimes I say something to her. It makes me feel as though her housework is more important than me.
III. Desirable or Positive Behaviors of Spouse
A. She is a good cook.
B. She works uncomplainingly.
C. Keeps house clean.
D. Very good mother to baby.
E. Very organized.
F. Dependable.
G. Thoughtful about many things.

The next step is quite different from what some would expect. This entails keeping a weeklong record of the number of times problem behavior number three—the least threatening behavior—occurs. This is not done to blame or react to your spouse, but to help each one become aware of his or her own reinforcing response to the behavior.

We begin with the least threatening behavior because it is easier to work out a mutual agreement with an easier problem. This should help any couple to proceed to the other more serious behaviors that need to be eliminated.

The way to eliminate a problem is to replace your reinforcing behaviors and increase the desired behaviors that your partner appreciates. Some partners verbally commit to each other that they will no longer respond the way they have, but let the problem behavior slide by. This takes patience, commitment, and prayer, but...it works.[2]

Foolish Questions

Remember when you were a child and your parents came into the room to break up a fight between you and a sibling or another child? What do you remember saying? What do kids say today when this happens? "He (or she) started it." And it continues throughout our lives. We get into a disagreement with our spouses and we either think or say, "You started it!" And if we verbalize it we usually frame it in the worst possible way by saying, "Why do you always have to start an argument?"

Fighting words. Ever said them? Ever heard them? "Why" is one of the worst ways to phrase a question. It puts the person on the defensive. Even if a person knew the answer to "why"—and often he or she doesn't—would he give the reason? And "always" is a gunpowder word. It's inflammatory. It incites a defensive posture, attitude, and response. And "have to" implies intent in a blaming way. You probably get the picture—bad phrasing of a question.

I don't think anyone is going to admit to starting the argument or fight anyway. Besides, regardless of who initiated it, would it continue if the other party didn't join in and participate? Not likely.

Instead of looking to see "who started it," what might happen if you concentrated more on "How did it end?" When you look at how disagreements end, you may find some solutions to use the next time and even shorten the disagreement. Learn from your solutions, achievements, and successes. For some it's when they say things like:

> "I see your point of view."
> "I guess I've never considered that."
> "I've never thought about it that way before."
> "I think I understand."
> "You're right."
> "I'm willing to give it a try."[3]

One of the principles I've learned about crises and losses in life is that eventually as people recover, they are able to discover something positive or beneficial from the experience amidst the pain and anguish. Sometimes it takes several months for the discovery to be made.

In marriage situations such as disagreements or hassles I think the discovery can be made earlier. The reason it often isn't is because we don't look for it. When a problem arises, instead of constantly looking for the negative outcome, look to see what is constructive about it. It may be there but either hidden or overlooked.

Some couples have discovered the following as expressed in their own words:

"We are more patient with one another after we confront a problem or have a disagreement."

"It takes me a while to see her point of view, but the only way I consider it is when we argue."

"I don't like getting angry, but I do feel better when I don't keep it bottled up."

"It's upsetting at the time but we sure become more intimate afterward."

THE POWER OF THE UNPREDICTABLE

Another way to bring out positive changes in a relationship is to do the unexpected. That is, doing something different when you know that what you're doing just isn't working. I learned about this in the early 1960s in a book I was reading in graduate school. The writer talked about it in relation to raising and disciplining children. Since I was a youth pastor at the time I wondered if it would work with teenagers and especially in large meetings.

Since most of us are predictable, and continue to respond in the same way (including me), I began to think, *When some kid begins to cut up and create a disturbance, how do I usually react? How do they expect me to respond?* Once I figured that out, I purposefully did something different. Because they weren't expecting it, they couldn't defend against it. I found that it worked. Then as I moved into counseling couples I wondered if it would work in their relationships. I experimented. It did.

Unexpected Tactics

Some of the unpredictable things I have seen couples do are as follows:

1. Instead of telling her husband not to get angry but to calm down (which never worked), a wife suggested that he needed to be angry and raise his voice. She pulled two chairs together and said, "Let's sit down and make it easier on ourselves." Interesting! He calmed down and sat down.

2. When a husband came in late occasionally because of traffic, instead of snapping at his wife when she complained that he should have called, he simply said, "Sorry," and gave her a tape that he had recorded in the car—complete with traffic noise—giving a report every five minutes of where he was and how fast the traffic was moving. There was no argument, and the next time he was late there was a different response from his wife.

3. Instead of telling her husband that he was yelling again (which he would always deny), a wife turned on a tape recorder in plain view of her husband. This did the trick and the yelling stopped. Not only then but the next time when he started to yell, as he saw the tape recorder he stopped yelling.

4. On a humorous note, a husband shared with me that he hated being predictable when he came into the house at night, so he thought up different ways of greeting each person when he arrived home. Some days he said he

would crawl in the doggy door and surprise everyone. He might surprise them, but he could get shot in the process!

A therapist who is one of the leaders of this approach shared one of her own family experiences:

> Knowing that a particular approach is entirely ineffective has no impact whatsoever on my choice of actions during subsequent crises. I find this to be a truly curious phenomenon. Consider what happened one evening at my house during dinnertime.
>
> Since I rarely prepare a homemade meal for dinner (my husband is the gourmet cook), I expect punctuality (and appreciation) when I do. Although my husband is generally considerate about informing me of his schedule, he occasionally "forgets," returning home later than usual without a phone call to advise me of his plans. There seems to be an uncanny correlation between the extremely infrequent occasions I decide to prepare a meal and his "forgetting" to come home on time.
>
> The sequence of events, when this occurs, is always the same. By the time he walks in, I have already tried calling several locations hoping to track him down. Dinner is ready and I mumble about the food getting cold. I suggest to my daughter that we begin without dad so that our food will still be hot. She senses my growing impatience. Later (what seems like years later) the door opens and I carefully plan my revenge—I will silently pout until he asks me, "What's wrong?" and then I will let him have it!
>
> As he enters the room he greets us and seats himself, commenting about how good dinner smells. Then he cordially obliges by asking, "What's wrong?" and I jump at the opportunity to tell him. He defends himself and accuses me of being unreasonable. Things generally deteriorate from there. This particular plan of attack never works. I know this but my behavior belies this awareness.
>
> However, something unusual happened one particular evening. The dinner scene was unfolding as usual when he walked through the door thirty minutes late. I was rehearsing to myself what I would say when he asked the million-dollar question. He predictably entered the room, said hello to us, sat down and began to eat. A couple of minutes passed and he did not inquire, "What's wrong?" "He's probably starving," I thought, reassuring myself that my attack was imminent. He then turned to my daughter and asked her how her day went in school. She launched into a ten-minute monologue consisting of

the longest sentence I have ever heard. I thought she would never stop talking. After all, I was still waiting for my invitation to explode.

When she finally finished, instead of addressing me, my husband began to tell her some details of his day at work. She listened politely as I felt rage building inside: "What nerve, he didn't ask me why I am pouting!" I waited a while longer though I couldn't help but become mildly interested in the conversation. Without realizing it I found myself joining the discussion. The remainder of the meal was very pleasant.

When I realized what had happened I asked my husband why he decided to talk to our daughter instead of asking about my silence. He replied, "You always tell your clients to do something different when they get stuck, but you never follow your own advice. I thought I would give it a shot." It's just awful to have your own weapons used against you![4]

Surprise Attacks

One of the most common conflicts I've heard is when a wife wants to share about her day with her husband, and the response is often not what she is looking for. Frequently, after about thirty seconds, when a husband realizes that this is going to take awhile, he tunes back into the TV or begins rereading his newspaper.

Why does this happen so much? Simply because most men need to have a goal or a focal point. While a wife is sharing her feelings, and especially if she isn't talking in a linear fashion, a man is looking for the main point or bottom line. When he realizes it's going to take awhile, he relaxes mentally and focuses on his viewing or reading. And many a man thinks he is still listening. Part of his mind is still with her. It's sort of scanning her words to see when she makes a point that calls for some response from him.

The typical—and worst—way a wife can respond is to confront her husband and say, "You're not listening!" This doesn't work for two good reasons. Many men heard this from their mothers, and now they feel they're being talked down to like a child again. They feel blamed. Second, they *do* hear their wives with a part of their minds. What they aren't doing is giving their full and individual attention—which is what wives really want. They want their husbands to reflect James 1:19 when it says to be "a ready listener" (*AMP*).

Wives usually do one of two things, or both. They attack with the "You're not listening" statement and/or walk away hurt and upset. Neither works.

Why not do the unpredictable? How? One way is to say what you really want and, if a husband is bottom line, put it in his language style. As one wife said, "Tom, when you begin looking at the newspaper again, I don't feel I have your full attention. That's what I really want from you. When you do I can share what I have to say much faster and more concisely. Then you can get back to your own reading or TV much quicker. And I'll feel good about it, too." I think most men will not only hear this, but understand.

Another wife did something totally different. When her husband turned away to read or look at the TV, she stopped too and just sat and waited. After awhile he realized she had stopped talking and he stopped and looked up. She said, "Thank you. I only need three to five minutes more and it helps me to have your full attention. Will that be all right with you?" This kind of approach usually gets the desired response. And whenever you get what you want, always thank the person.[5]

The Forgetfulness Fight

Another common issue in marriage is "remembering and forgetting"—one partner asks the other to do something and the partner forgets. The opportunity to attack presents itself and the partner who forgot responds in a defensive and protective way.

You've probably asked questions like "Did you pick up the dry cleaning?" (or books at the library, photos, my prescription, bread, milk, etc.). That's a good question. It's positive. Much better than "I hope you didn't forget to ..." or "I didn't see what I asked you to get and I was clear about how important it was. Did you forget again?"

Once you've asked in a positive way, respond in the same way if your spouse hasn't done it, with statements like "That's OK." "It's no problem." "Maybe we can get it tomorrow." If there is a time pressure ask a question that solves a problem and can lead to a solution:

"Honey, we need it tonight. Do you have any suggestions?"

"Honey, we need it tonight. Do you want to run back for it? Or I could if you can take over this project."

"Since we need it for this evening, I wonder if you could call one of the other couples to bring it?"

Whatever you do, do something different if your usual response doesn't work.

ACCENTUATE THE POSITIVE

If you want your marriage to grow, focus on solutions, not just the problems. That's the message of this chapter. Switch the use of your imagination to a positive direction rather than a negative focus. I think most people create complete full-length mental pictures of themselves engaging in marital combat with their spouses, and thus they are prone to make that a reality. When you use the same energy and time to focus your imagination and concentration on what's working as well as the solution, you begin to expect that to happen. Act as if it is going to happen and talk as if it is going to be a reality.

This is nothing new. This procedure has been refined in the field of sports, especially tennis, racquetball, bobsledding, and skiing. In skiing, for example, the athletes will stand at the top of the ski run, close their eyes, and make the downhill run step by step in their minds. They see themselves making the precise moves at the right time as fast as possible. You actually see their bodies bob and weave as they go through the run in their minds.

I've used this rehearsal technique when playing racquetball, especially if I'm making bad shots and losing. When I concentrate on what I'm doing wrong, I continue to lose. But when I remember to concentrate on what works and what I will be doing in the next shot, I play better. It's as simple as that.

This is an important principle in your marriage, too. Concentrate on what you will be doing either differently or positively. Then commit it to prayer—don't attempt to do it without the Lord's guidance and power. When you visualize your intent to be different or loving or accepting, you move toward that reality.

Perhaps it would be helpful to look at your marriage now, and consider what you like about your relationship that you would like to see continue. Talk together about what you can do to ensure that it does continue.

As you can see, everything suggested in this chapter is simple. Not at all profound. But over the years I've wondered why more couples don't follow these principles. As one husband put it, "Norm, I just never thought about it like that before. Now that I do, it makes sense."

I think the potential for what can happen is summarized in this poem:

I will be with you
no matter what happens
to us and between us.
If you should become blind tomorrow,
I will be there.
If you achieve no success
and attain no status in our society,
I will be there.

When we argue and are angry,
as we inevitably will,
I will work to bring us together.
When we seem totally at odds
and neither of us is having needs fulfilled,
I will persist in trying to understand
and in trying to restore our relationship.

When our marriage seems utterly sterile
and going nowhere at all,
I will believe that it can work,
and I will want it to work,
and I will do my part to make it work.

And when all is wonderful
and we are happy,
I will rejoice over our life together,
and continue to strive
to keep our relationship growing and strong.[6]

NOTES

1. Clifford Notarious and Howard Markman, *We Can Work It Out* (New York: G. P. Putnam's Sons, 1993), pp. 70–73, adapted.
2. Alan S. Gurman and David G. Rice, *Couples in Conflict* (New York: Jason Aronson, Inc., 1975), pp. 268–269, adapted from "A Behavioral Exchange Model for Marital Counseling" by Alan F. Rappaport and Janet E. Harrel.
3. Michelle Weiner–Davis, *Divorce Busting* (New York: Simon & Schuster, 1992), pp. 130–133, 126–128, adapted.
4. Ibid., pp. 148–149.
5. John Gray, *What Your Mother Couldn't Tell You and Your Father Didn't Know* (New York: HarperCollins, 1994), pp. 176–179, adapted.
6. Elizabeth Achtemeier, *The Committed Marriage* (Philadelphia: Westminster Press, 1976), p. 41.

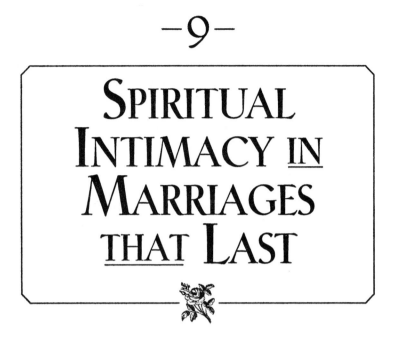

-9-

SPIRITUAL INTIMACY IN MARRIAGES THAT LAST

The young woman in my office was animated, though not so upset. "I never dreamed what has happened in our marriage during the past year was possible," she said. "We've gone along for years just sort of ho-hum. Nothing bad, nothing spectacular—just steady. I guess we were in a rut. It was comfortable, and I guess we felt, or I did, that this was the way it would always be. But Jim came home from that men's conference and made all kinds of changes. Even though they were mostly positive, it took me awhile to adjust.

"The first thing he did was come up to me and apologize for not telling me that he prayed for me every day, and had for years. How would I have ever known?! In fact, that's what I started to say, but I caught myself and thanked him for telling me. A week later he 'casually' asked me how I would feel about praying together and reading from the Bible occasionally. I have to laugh now because it's like he wanted me to but wasn't sure how I would respond. So we did.

"I can't explain why or what happened, but there is this incredible sense of bonding or closeness now that we never had before. We pray, we read, we share. Sometimes I call him and pray a sentence prayer for him over the phone. He does the same. And our sex life is a whole different story. Others have seen our relationship change. And when they ask, we tell them. I guess we're finally experiencing what the Bible says about cleaving in the full sense of the word."

Spiritual bonding. Spiritual intimacy. Spiritual closeness. Desired, yet avoided. Available, yet illusive for so many.

Difficult, but Desired

When partners are asked the question "How close are you spiritually as a couple?" there are usually two responses. Many say, "We're not spiritually close," or "We're not as close as we could be." The second response is, "I think we would like to be." Many couples, when they finally talk about it, discover they would like to be closer spiritually, but they were uncomfortable dealing with it. It was difficult, so it was never discussed.

I hear couples say, "We need to. We want to. We don't." What keeps us from developing this area that can bring an even greater depth to the other dimensions of intimacy?

Some couples say, "We really don't know any couples who do, and we're not exactly sure how to go about it." Perhaps there is a lack of role models for us to follow because we don't ask others what they do. We would be embarrassed if asked, so we feel others would be as well. And we avoid putting them on the spot.

Still other couples say, "We just don't have time. With our schedules we hardly have enough time to say 'hello' to each other, let alone have devotions together."

To relate together spiritually means creatively meshing two people's schedules. And yet, we have the greatest time-saving gadgets. When either an individual or a couple states they don't have time to develop the spiritual intimacy in their marriage, I say, "I don't agree. I've never met anyone who couldn't work out the time. It may take some creative juggling, but it's a choice—like so much of the rest of life. You have to be flexible, committed, and have realistic expectations for what you want to have happen in the relationship."

Others have said, "We're not at the same place spiritually in order to share this together." Perhaps praying or reading the Bible together would be the very process that would enable them to become more unified spiritually.

Some people have simply asked, "Why? Why develop this? Why do this? I'm not sure of the benefits." If a couple says this to me I won't even debate the issue with them or try to convince them. But I can say this to them: "I don't know if anyone could really explain why or convince you. Perhaps the best way to discover the benefits is just to try it for a week. Then evaluate the process to see if it does anything for you. Anyone can give one week of his or her life for an experiment such as this."

The Risk of Isolation

People can have strong, individual, personal relationships with the Lord, but never invite their partners into their lives to experience the spiritual journey together. When one partner wants this and the other resists overtly or just drags his or her feet, it can have a damaging effect upon the relationship. A friend of mine shared his experience before he and his wife decided to develop this dimension of their relationship:

> When it came to the day to day sharing of our own spiritual journeys (the real test of spiritual intimacy), it wasn't there. Privacy was the rule.
>
> Jan would want us to read something together, and I would be too busy. She would want us to pray, and I would be too tired. She would share something deeply personal, but I would not respond. I would listen intently, but my sympathetic stares were followed with deafening silence. On the rare occasions when I did respond, it was only with a summarization of what she had said, an acknowledgment, but never a personal reflection.
>
> To Jan, my avoidant behavior communicated that I was not interested in spiritual matters and, to some extent, that I did not care about her needs. Gradually my excuses and my silence took their toll and she tired of her efforts. The requests for my involvement, the statements of her need, the times of her own personal sharing—all of these tapered off. Jan seemed to resign herself to the fact that it just was not going to happen. For whatever reason, we were not going to be spiritually intimate. Our sharing would be limited to crises.
>
> With Jan's resignation came some resentment. This was not a seething-caldron type of problem, but on occasion it would become clear that "resignation" had not brought "resolution." Jan still desired the closeness that was missing, and the disappointment was frustrating.[1]

Many marriage partners today feel close to their spouses in every way except spiritually. In that area they feel isolated. Often this isolation cannot be kept in check, and it may creep into other areas of a couple's life and impact those areas, too. And the more one person wants to be close spiritually and the other resists, the more resentment will build.

Many couples find themselves in this bind, but it can be overcome.

SHARING YOUR "INMOST"

What is spiritual intimacy? For that matter, what is intimacy? There is a great deal of confusion about this word because so many people think it simply refers to a sexual relationship. The word actually comes from a Latin word, *intimus*, meaning "inmost."

Intimacy suggests a very strong personal relationship, a special emotional closeness that includes understanding and being understood by someone who is very special. Intimacy has also been defined as an affectionate bond, the strands of which are composed of mutual caring, responsibility, trust, open communication of feelings and sensations, and the nondefended interchange of information about significant emotional events. Intimacy means taking the risk to be close to someone and allowing that someone to step inside your personal boundaries.

Sometimes intimacy can hurt. As you lower your defenses to let each other close, you reveal the real, intimate, secret you to each other, including your weaknesses and faults. With the real you exposed, you become vulnerable to possible ridicule from your partner. The risk of pain is there, but the rewards of intimacy greatly overshadow the risk.

Although intimacy means vulnerability, it also means security. The openness can be scary, but the acceptance each partner offers in the midst of vulnerability provides a wonderful sense of security. Intimate couples can feel safe and accepted—fully exposed perhaps, yet fully accepted.

Intimacy can occur outside of marriage commitment and without the element of physical love. Women can be intimate with women and men with men. The closeness of intimacy involves private and personal interaction, commitment, and caring. We can speak of intimacy between friends as well as intimacy between spouses.

Intimacy can exist without marriage, but it is impossible for a meaningful marriage to exist without intimacy. For two hearts to touch each other, intimacy is a must. If you don't know how your partner thinks and feels about various issues or concerns, he or she is somewhat of a stranger to you. And for two hearts to be bonded together, they cannot be strangers.

It is often assumed that intimacy automatically occurs between married partners. But I've seen far too many "married strangers." I've talked to too many husbands and wives who feel isolated from their spouses and lonely even after many years of marriage. I've heard statements like:

"We share the same house, the same table, and the same bed, but we might as well be strangers."

"We've lived together for twenty-three years, and yet I don't know my spouse any better now than when we married."

"What really hurts is that we can spend a weekend together and I still feel lonely. I think I married someone who would have preferred being a hermit in some ways."

No, intimacy is not automatic.

DIMENSIONS OF INTIMACY

Actually there are several dimensions of intimacy. It's not limited to one quality such as sex. Several elements are involved in creating an intimate relationship. Many relationships have gaps in them for one reason or another. You may be close in two or three areas but distant in others. If you feel you have a close, intimate relationship, but you're distant in a couple of them or even one, there is work to be done. Let's consider the various dimensions before looking at the spiritual aspect, because they all relate.

Emotional intimacy is the foundation for relating in a couple's relationship. There is a "feeling" of closeness when this exists, a mutual feeling of care and support coming from each person. You share everything in the emotional arena, including your hurts and your joys. You understand each other, and you're attentive to your spouse's feelings.

Social intimacy involves having friends in common rather than always socializing separately. Having mutual friends to play with, talk with, pray with, and give reciprocal support to is reflective of this important dimension.

Sexual intimacy is taken for granted in marriage. Many couples have sex but no sexual intimacy. Performing a physical act is one thing, but communicating about it is another. Sexual intimacy involves satisfaction with what occurs. But it also means you talk about it, endeavor to meet your partner's needs, and keep it from being routine. There is an understanding of each other's unique gender needs, and flexibility in meeting them.

There is even the dimension of *intellectual* intimacy—the sharing of ideas and the stimulation of each other's level of knowledge and understanding. You are each different, and you have grown because of what your partner has shared with you.

Joyce and I have become much more involved this way in the last ten years of our marriage. We share or point out some idea or save something we learned in an article, book, newscast, or TV program. We value each other's opinion. For this dimension to exist, you need mutual respect. You cannot be threatened by the sharing, but must value what's given.

Recreational intimacy means you share and enjoy the same interests and activities. You just like to play together, and it doesn't have to be competitive. You have fun together, and it draws you closer together.

SHARING YOUR SPIRITUAL SELVES

Then we come to *spiritual* intimacy. Just to keep everything in balance, even though this dimension may be more significant than others, you need the others in order to be complete, too. I've seen some couples who have spiritual intimacy but lack social and recreational. That's out of balance.[2]

In his book *The Spiritually Intimate Marriage*, Don Harvey has the most complete definition that I've found. He says spiritual intimacy is:

Being able to *share* your spiritual self, find this reciprocated, and have a sense of union with your mate.

Based on this definition, spiritual intimacy is something that we do, something that we feel, and something that is *interactional*.

Sharing is something that we do; it is a behavior. It is an act of self-disclosure, of opening yourself up to someone else and privileging them with a genuine glimpse of who you really are. The variety of what can be shared is enormous. At one time it may be more of a cognitive nature: You may share your beliefs and insights. Or, delving a little deeper, you may share your misbeliefs: your doubts and apprehensions. At times you will share your feelings. This will include both the good (joy and peace) and the bad (fear and pain). There will be times of victory and growth, and there will be times of dismay, when burdens, struggles, and seeming failure weigh you down. All of this represents your spiritual self, and this is what is shared in an intimate relationship.

A sense of union is emotional. It is something that we feel. There is a sense of acceptance, of being known for who you really are and knowing that is okay. You know that you are cared for spiritually, that at least one person is praying for you. With this sense of union is the feeling that you are spiritually "in tune" as a couple—that this is truly a marriage.

Finally, to *find it reciprocated* implies an interactional element. You cannot stand alone and experience intimacy. That is isolation. Intimacy is not a one-person game; it requires two of you. Depthful sharing that is not reciprocated by a mate will not lead to closeness. There must be an effort by you and your mate if intimacy is to be approached. It takes two.[3]

I know couples who worship regularly together, but there is no spiritual intimacy. I know couples who read the Scripture regularly together, but have no spiritual intimacy. I know couples who pray and share together sporadically, but are lacking in spiritual intimacy. I know some couples who don't pray and share, yet have spiritual intimacy.

What's the difference? It seems to be in their attitudes. Spiritual intimacy is a heart's desire to be close to God and submit to His direction for your lives. It is the willingness to seek His guidance together, to allow the teaching of His Word in your everyday life. It's a willingness to allow God to help you overcome your sense of discomfort over sharing spiritually and learn to see your marriage together as a spiritual adventure. It's a willingness to enthrone

Jesus Christ as Lord of your lives and to look to Him for direction in your decisions, such as which house to buy, where to go on vacations, or which school is best for the children. It means He will direct both of you, and change your hearts to be in agreement rather than speak just through one of you.

Lordship and Control

Spiritual intimacy in marriage requires both partners to submit to the leadership and lordship of Christ, instead of competing for control. One author wrote:

> We can gather all the facts needed in making a decision. We can thresh out our differences as to the shape and direction our decision should take. We can put off the decision while we allow the relevant information to simmer in our minds. Even then, however, we may be uneasy: we still don't know what is best to do, and the right decision just won't come.
>
> When we turn to the Lord Jesus Christ and open our consciences to His Spirit's leading, some new events, remembrances, and forgotten facts will come to us. A whole new pattern will emerge. We can then move with abandon in a whole new direction which we had not previously considered. Looking back, we may conclude that God's providence delivered us from what would have been the worst possible decision. Jesus as Lord made the difference between deliverance and destruction.[4]

When Jesus is Lord of your marriage, it relieves you of the problem of experiencing a power struggle. Jesus expressed something interesting to His disciples when He said, "You know that those who are regarded as rulers of the Gentiles lord it over them, and their high officials exercise authority over them. Not so with you. Instead, whoever wants to become great among you must be your servant" (Mark 10:42,43, *NIV*).

Earlier we talked about the dominant–submissive relationship, and how intimacy cannot develop in this style of marriage. It's true for spiritual intimacy as well.

I've seen marriages in which one member dictates the spiritual dimension by selecting the church they attend, the meetings attended, what magazines and books are allowed, as well as which Bible version is the accepted one! It's difficult to see how this reflects Paul's words: "Outdo one another in showing honor" (Rom. 12:10, *RSV*) to each other.

Even in a spiritually intimate marriage, faith differences may surface occasionally, but that's normal. With tolerance for diversity couples can have a shared faith relationship that includes his faith, her faith, and their faith.

Requirements for Spiritual Intimacy

Some couples seem to be able to develop spiritual intimacy and others never do. What makes the difference? Spiritual intimacy has the opportunity to grow in a relationship that has a degree of stability. When the two of you experience trust, honesty, open communication, and dependability, you are more willing to risk being vulnerable spiritually. Creating this dimension will increase the stability factor as well.

For a couple to have spiritual intimacy they need shared beliefs as to who Jesus is and the basic tenets of the Christian faith. You may have different beliefs about the second coming of Christ, or whether all the spiritual gifts are for today or not. One of you may enjoy an informal church service while the other likes a high church formal service, or one of you may be charismatic and the other not. It's important that your beliefs are important to you. You've made them something personal and significant for your life. There can still be spiritual intimacy within this diversity.

We hear about mismatched couples when one is a Christian and one isn't. You can also have a mismatch when both are believers but one wants to grow, and is growing, and the other doesn't and isn't![5]

A wonderful way to encourage spiritual intimacy is to share the history of your spiritual life. Many couples know where their spouses are currently, but very little of how they came to that place.

Use the following questions to discover more about your partner's faith:

1. What did your parents believe about God, Jesus, church, prayer, the Bible?

2. What was your definition of being spiritually alive?

3. Which parent did you see as being spiritually alive?

4. What specifically did each teach you directly and indirectly about spiritual matters?

5. Where did you first learn about God? About Jesus? About the Holy Spirit? What age?

6. What was your best experience in church as a child? As a teen?

7. What was your worst experience in church as a child? As a teen?

8. Describe your conversion experience. When? Who was involved? Where?

9. If possible, describe your baptism. What did it mean to you?

10. Which Sunday School teacher influenced you the most? In what way?

11. Which minister influenced you the most? In what way?

12. What questions did you have as a child/teen about your faith? Who gave you any answers?

13. Was there any camp or special meetings that affected you spiritually?

14. Did you read the Bible as a teen?
15. Did you memorize any Scripture as a child or teen? Do you remember any now?
16. As a child, if you could have asked God any questions, what would they have been?
17. As a teen, if you could have asked God any questions, what would they have been?
18. If you could ask God any questions now, what would they be?
19. What would have helped you more spiritually when you were growing up?
20. Did anyone disappoint you spiritually as a child? If so, how has that impacted you as an adult?
21. When you went through difficult times as a child or teen, how did that affect your faith?
22. What has been the greatest spiritual experience of your life?

The Gift of Praying Together

How important is prayer together as a couple? Vital. No other way to put it. It's vital. Think of praying together as a couple not as a duty, a drudgery, or a negative mandate. It is a gift from Him. Over the years I've collected statements or quotes from others whose words have encouraged and challenged me in my own marriage. Reflect on the following statements about prayer. Consider their truth. Explore how they can infuse your life with a new depth of togetherness and closeness.

> Prayer is an awareness of the presence of a holy and loving God in one's life, and an awareness of God's relations to one's husband or wife. Prayer is listening to God, a valuable lesson in learning to listen to one another. In prayer one searches the interior life for blocks to personal surrender to God, evaluating one's conduct in the quiet of prayerful meditation. At times prayer may be rich with confession and self-humbling, or with renunciation and higher resolve to fulfill God's best. Praying together shuts out the petty elements of daily conflict and anxiety, permitting a couple to gain a higher perspective upon their lives, allowing their spirits to be elevated to a consideration of eternal values and enduring relationships. Prayer helps a couple sort out unworthy objects of concern and helps them to concentrate on the nobler goals of life. All the threatening things that trouble a pair can find relief in the presence of God; humbling themselves before Him, they humble themselves before one another—an invaluable therapy. In this way the couple comes to

honest estimates of themselves and one another. Unbecoming self-assurance and stubborn independence give way before the recognition of their inadequacy to meet divine standards of life; thus, two people are led to seek God's help and the support of each other.[6]

It is only when a husband and wife pray together before God that they find the secret of true harmony, that the difference in their temperaments, their ideas, and their tastes enriches their home instead of endangering it. There will be no further question of one imposing his will on the other, or of the other giving in for the sake of peace. Instead, they will together seek God's will, which alone will ensure that each will be fully able to develop his personality....When each of the marriage partners seeks quietly before God to see his own faults, recognizes his sin, and asks the forgiveness of the other, marital problems are no more. Each learns to speak the other's language, and to meet him halfway, so to speak. Each holds back those harsh little words which one is apt to utter when one is right, but which are said in order to injure. Most of all, a couple rediscovers complete mutual confidence, because, in meditating in prayer together, they learn to become absolutely honest with each other....This is the price to be paid if partners very different from each other are to combine their gifts instead of setting them against each other.[7]

Lines open to God are invariably open to one another for a person cannot be genuinely open to God and closed to his mate. Praying together especially reduces the sense of competitiveness in marriage, at the same time enhancing the sense of complementarity and completeness. The Holy Spirit seeks only the opportunity to minister to whatever needs are present in a marriage, and in their moments of prayer together a couple gives Him entrance into opened hearts and minds. God fulfills His design for Christian marriage when lines of communication are first opened to Him.[8]

There is a sense in which marriage is a three-story affair. There is a third floor of the spiritual where we worship together, where we appreciate God together, where we pray together. If we disagree here, a certain disunity will seep down into the second floor, which is our emotional and mental state. This will lead us to disputes, mental and intellectual debating and haggling; and this division on the second floor naturally seeps down into the physical relations of the first floor and takes the deepest desire from them. Everything that is crowned is crowned from above! Unless in the marriage relationship there is an "above", some spiritual rapport, it is difficult for the physical relationship to be at its best.[9]

Scripture also tells us to pray:

> "As for me, far be it from me that I should sin against the Lord by ending my prayers for you; and I will continue to teach you those things which are good and right" (1 Sam. 12:23, *TLB*).

> "You haven't tried this before, [but begin now]. Ask, using my name, and you will receive, and your cup of joy will overflow" (John 16:24, *TLB*).

> Don't worry about anything; instead, pray about everything; tell God your needs and don't forget to thank him for his answers (Phil. 4:6, *TLB*).

> Always keep on praying (1 Thess. 5:17, *TLB*).

> Admit your faults to one another and pray for each other so that you may be healed. The earnest prayer of a righteous man has great power and wonderful results (James 5:16, *TLB*).

How to Start

How do you start praying together as a couple? Why not begin by praying by yourself for your partner? Do it daily, earnestly, hopefully, specifically. Ask God to bless and to lead your spouse. I know couples who call one another during the day to tell them they're praying for each other. Other couples ask each other before they part for the day, "How can I pray for you today?" At the conclusion of the day, it gives you something to discuss. When I'm on a trip, I've found notes in my clothes from Joyce stating that she is praying for me.

The easiest way to begin praying together is to take the time and set a time to do it. I've heard so many say that with their schedules it's almost impossible. I disagree. Creativity and flexibility can make it happen. You can put your arms around each other for thirty seconds and pray before you leave for the day or after dinner. Couples can pray together over the phone when they're apart. Creative couples write their prayers and send them to each other via the fax machine. With cellular phones couples can pray while driving (hopefully with their eyes open) and make contact in this way.

When you start praying together at home, perhaps it's best just to share some requests, then pray silently together. There is no threat to this.

Praying aloud is something you grow into. It may take a while to develop a comfort level. Communication doesn't always have to be vocal. We're bombarded with noise all the time. Sometimes couples struggle with audible prayer, because they don't communicate very much with each other on anything else. Or one spouse feels that the other is much more articulate and fluent. It could be true, but this is not a time for comparison or competitive endeavor. It's a time for learning to accept who you are. I've always felt my wife's prayers were much more detailed and in-depth than mine. But this has never hindered me from praying aloud.

I like the journey that Charles and Martha Shedd experienced in learning to pray together.

> We would sit on our rocking love seat. We would take turns telling each other things we'd like to pray about. Then holding hands we would pray each in our own way, silently.
>
> This was the beginning of prayer together that lasted. Naturally, through the years we've learned to pray in every possible way, including aloud. Anytime, anywhere, every position, every setting, in everyday language. Seldom with "thee" or "thou." Plain talk. Ordinary conversation. We interrupt, we laugh, we argue, we enjoy. We hurt together, cry together, wonder together. Together we tune our friendship to the Friend of friends.
>
> Do we still pray silently together? Often. Some groanings of the spirit go better in the silence.
>
> "I've been feeling anxious lately and I don't know why. Will you listen while I tell you what I can? Then let's pray about the known and unknown in silence."
>
> "This is one of my super days. So good. Yet somehow I can't find words to tell you. Let's thank the Lord together in the quiet."
>
> Negatives, positives, woes, celebrations, shadowy things—all these, all kinds of things we share in prayer. Aloud we share what we can. Without the vocals we share those things not ready yet for words.
>
> Why would this approach have the feel of the real? Almost from the first we knew we'd discovered an authentic new dimension.
>
> In becoming best friends with each other, we were becoming best friends with the Lord.

And the more we sought his friendship, the more we were becoming best friends with each other.[10]

What God Does Through Couples' Prayers

One of the other reasons for praying silently has to do with the unique way God has created us in both our gender and personality differences. Most men prefer to put things on the back burner and think about them for awhile. Thus, if a man has the opportunity to reflect on what he wants to pray about, he would eventually be more open to praying. Extroverts find it easier to pray aloud because they think out loud; whereas introverts need to think things through silently in their minds before sharing. Silent prayer is less threatening. Some prefer reflecting for awhile first and writing out their prayer. There is nothing wrong with this.

There are numerous benefits from praying together. When a man and woman marry they no longer think and act as a single person. It is no longer "I" but "we." All of life is then lived in connection with another person. Everything you do affects this significant person. You're a team of two, and when both of you participate, you function better. When you confront problems and crises in your life (and you will), it's a tremendous source of comfort and support to know that here is another person who will pray for you and with you. When you're struggling financially, or with problems at work, when you have tough decisions to make, or a medical crisis, to be able to share the burden with your spouse lightens the load.

Couples need to pray together for the health of their marriages. When you married, you entered into a high-risk adventure. The vows you took at your wedding will be attacked on all sides. Praying together will make your marriage stronger as well as help to protect you from reacting sinfully toward your spouse.

Scripture's promise about the effectiveness of prayer includes the prayers of married couples. Jesus said, "Again, I tell you that if two of you on earth agree about anything you ask for, it will be done for you by my Father in heaven. For where two or three come together in my name, there am I with them" (Matt. 18:19,20, *NIV*).

Couples who have prayer lists and see the results of answered prayer will be encouraged as they see how God works in their lives.

When couples pray together it has an impact on disagreements, conflicts, and anger expressed toward each other. When you see your spouse as a child of God, valuable and precious in His sight, someone He sent His Son to die for, wouldn't that have an effect on how you pray for him or her? In the book *If Two Shall Agree* by Carey Moore and Pamela Roswell Moore, Carey puts it plainly:

To place Christ at the center of our homes means, of course, to tell Him, "You are our God," not just at prayer time but all day long. I cannot be careless or insensitive in what I say to Pam and then pray with her. Nor can either of us treat anyone else rudely or engage in gossip and criticism or allow conceit and pride to rule our relations with others, and expect God to hear our prayers at the end of the day.

Praying together involves the family finances, how we spend our time, what we do for entertainment, the thoughts we dwell upon when we are apart. I cannot be dishonest or profligate or stingy in money matters and then pray with my wife for His blessing on our economic life. Nor can we be cavalier with the way we spend money on clothes or a vacation or a new car, and then pray for the poor. I cannot harbor jealousy or hatred or lust or self-conceit in my thoughts, nor can Pam, and then expect God to hear us as we pray. When we come into His presence God searches our hearts. "Surely you desire truth in the inner parts" (Psalm 51:6)."

Help from the Holy Spirit

Have you ever felt like this when it comes to prayer?—"I just don't know what to say when I pray. Sometimes I'm at a loss for words."

If you've ever felt this way, you're not alone. We've all felt like this at some point. Often it's when we attempt to pray that we become very conscious of a spiritual struggle in our lives. As we sit down to pray, our minds wander. Every few minutes we sneak a look at the clock to see if we've prayed enough. Has that happened to you when you pray alone? It has to me. But it's interesting that when couples pray together it happens less often.

The Holy Spirit is God's answer when we don't know how to pray. You and I cannot pray as we ought to pray. We are often crippled in our prayer lives. That's where the work of the Holy Spirit really comes into play. He helps us in our prayer lives by showing us what we should pray for and how we ought to pray. That's quite a promise!

J. B. Phillips translates Romans 8:26,27 in this manner:

> The Spirit of God not only maintains this type within us, but helps us in our present limitations. For example, we do not know how to pray worthily as sons of God, but his Spirit within us is actually praying for us in those agonizing longings which never find words. And God who knows the heart's secrets understands, of course, the Spirit's intention as he prays for those who love God.

One of your callings in marriage is to assist your partner when he or she needs help. You are always to be listening for a call for assistance. Similarly, there is someone looking out for us when we need help in our prayer lives: the Holy Spirit. There are several specific ways that He helps us.

First, *the Spirit intercedes for you* when you are oppressed by problems in life or when you feel down on yourself. He brings you to the place where you can pray. Your ability to begin praying is prompted and produced by the working of the Holy Spirit within you. There may be times when all you can do is sigh or sob inwardly. Even this kind of prayer is the result of the Spirit's work.

Second, *the Spirit reveals to your mind what you should pray for*. He makes you conscious of such things as your needs, your lack of faith, your fears, your need to be obedient, etc. He helps you identify your spiritual needs and bring them into the presence of God. He helps you by diminishing your fears, increasing your faith, and strengthening your hope. If you're at a loss to know what you need to pray for about your partner or even what to pray for together, ask the Holy Spirit to intercede for you.

Third, *the Spirit guides you by directing your thoughts* to the promises of God's Word that are best suited to your needs. He helps you realize the truth of God's promises. The discernment that you lack on your own is supplied to you by the Spirit. Perhaps you're looking for a verse to apply to your marriage. Again, help is available through the Spirit.

Finally, *the Spirit helps you pray in the right way*. He helps you sift through your prayers and bring them into conformity with the purpose of prayer.

When you experience a crisis, it may be difficult for you to talk. But you and your spouse can hold each other in your arms and quietly allow the Holy Spirit to pray for you. This is called the silent prayer of the heart.

When you are having difficulty praying, remember that you have someone to draw on for strength in developing your prayer life.

Keeping Your Appointment with God

When is the best time for a couple to pray? You decide for yourself. It may vary or it may be set. There will be all kinds of interferences from the phone and TV, and child interruptions and exhaustion. But a commitment to be faithful in prayer can override excuses. Jim Dobson shares a situation he and his wife, Shirley, experienced:

> I'll never forget the time a few years ago when our daughter had just learned to drive....It was during this era that Shirley and I covenanted between us to pray for our son and daughter at the close of every day. Not only were we concerned about the risk of an automobile accident, but we were also aware of so many

other dangers that lurk out there in a city like Los Angeles....That's one reason we found ourselves on our knees each evening, asking for divine protection for the teenagers whom we love so much.

One night we were particularly tired and collapsed into bed without our benedictory prayer. We were almost asleep before Shirley's voice pierced the night. "Jim," she said. "We haven't prayed for our kids yet today."

I admit it was very difficult for me to pull my 6'2" frame out of the warm bed that night. Nevertheless, we got on our knees and offered a prayer for our children's safety, placing them in the hands of the Father once more.

Later we learned that [our daughter] Danae and a girl friend had gone to a fast-food establishment and bought hamburgers and Cokes. They drove up the road a few miles and were sitting in the car eating the meal when a policeman drove by, shining his spotlight in all directions, obviously looking for someone.

In a few minutes, Danae and her friend heard a "clunk" from under the car. They looked at one another nervously and felt another sharp bump. Then a man crawled out from under the car. He was unshaven and looked like he had been on the street for weeks. He tugged at the door attempting to open it. Thank God, it was locked. Danae quickly started the car and drove off...no doubt at record speed.

Later, when we checked the timing of this incident, we realized that Shirley and I had been on our knees at the precise moment of danger. Our prayers were answered. Our daughter and her friend were safe![12]

We keep appointments with others, and make sure we're always available for certain TV shows. Similarly, when you establish a specific time or pattern for prayer and keep to it consistently it becomes a regular part of your life. Some couples pray in their kitchens, family rooms, bedrooms, cars, or on walks. Work out what's best for you.

The Content of Your Prayers

Sometimes it helps to read prayers out loud that others have written. For years (even since college!) off and on I've used a book of daily prayers by John Baille called *A Diary of Private Prayer*. Reading the Psalms aloud can be a prayer. You can pray about everything and I mean everything.

Recently I found a fascinating resource that personalizes passages of Scripture into prayers for a husband and wife. It's called *Praying God's Will for My Marriage* by Lee Roberts. It simply takes passages of Scripture and rewords them. By reading these aloud for awhile, any couple could learn to do this for themselves. Here is a sampling:

> I pray that my spouse and I will be swift to hear, slow to speak, slow to wrath: for the wrath of man does not produce the righteousness of God (James 1:19–20).

> I pray that my spouse and I will always love the Lord our God with all our heart, with all our soul, with all our mind, and with all our strength and that we love our neighbor as ourselves (Mark 12:30–31).

> I pray that when my spouse and I face an obstacle we always remember that God has said, "Not by might nor by power, but by my Spirit" (Zechariah 4:6).

> I pray that if my spouse and I lack wisdom, we ask it of You, God, who gives to all liberally and without reproach and that it will be given to us (James 1:5).

> I pray that because freely my spouse and I have received, freely we will give (Matthew 10:8).

> I pray, O God, that You have comforted my spouse and me and will have mercy on our afflictions (Isaiah 49:13).

> I pray that my spouse and I will bless You, the Lord, at all times; and that Your praise continually be in our mouths (Psalm 34:1).

> I pray to You, God, that my spouse and I will present our bodies a living sacrifice, holy and acceptable to God, which is our reasonable service. I pray also that we will not be conformed to this world, but transformed by the renewing of our minds, that we may prove what is that good and acceptable and perfect will of God (Romans 12:1–2).[13]

Can you imagine the effect on your relationship when you literally bathe yourselves with God's Word as a prayer? Try this for a one-month experiment. Then note the difference in your marriage.

Prayer is one of the best ways to experience closeness. When your partner is discouraged, go up to him/her and hug him/her, and pray a one-line prayer of support. You can do this with your eyes open and looking him/her in the face. When he/she is upset or stressed, you could touch him/her on the arm and pray, "Lord, give strength and peace, lift the pressure, and show me how to support my loved one." This in itself can be supportive.

Before or after making love you could thank God for your spouse's love and physical attributes as well as for the gift of sex. Praying about sex? Why not? It's God's idea. It's His creation. It's His gift. How would you like to pray the following prayer?

> Thank you, O Redeemer,
> > for letting me express love through sex.
> Thank you for making it possible
> > for things to be right with sex—
> > that there can be beauty and wonder
> > between woman and man.
> You have given us a model for love in Jesus.
> He lived and laughed and accepted his humanity.
> He resisted sexual temptations
> Which were every bit as real as mine.
> He taught about the relationship of husband and wife
> > By showing love for his bride the church.
> Thank you that he gives me
> > the power to resist temptations also.
> Thank you that real sexual freedom
> > comes in being bound to the true man Jesus.
> Everywhere there are signs that point to the sex god:
> > Books declare that sex is our savior;
> > Songs are sung as prayers to sex;
> > Pictures show its airbrushed incantations;
> > Advertisers hawk its perfume and after-shave
> > libations.
> Help me know that sex is not salvation.
> Help me see instead that there is salvation for sex.
> For the exciting sensations of erotic love,
> > I offer you my thanks.
> For the affirmation of self-giving love,
> > I offer you my thanks.
> Lord, you replace sexual boredom with joy;
> > You point past sexual slavery to the hope of purity;
> > You enable sexual lovers to be friends;
> > You teach how to replace lust-making with
> > lovemaking.

Would I have any hope for sexual responsibility
Without the power you give?
Would I ever be a covenant keeper
Without the fidelity you inspire?
Thank you, Lord, for a love that stays when the bed
    is made.
Help me to keep my marriage bed undefiled—
    To see it as an altar of grace and pleasure.
Keep sex good in my life,
    Through your redeeming love.
Teach me to say:
    "Thank God for sex!"[14]

Testimonies About Couples' Prayers

What has prayer done for couples? Listen to some of these testimonies:

"We both feel that communication with God deepens...the spiritual and emotional intimacy we share with one another," one couple wrote. "Prayer is the means by which we build upon the Lord's love for us as the foundation of our marriage, and the medium by which we achieve spiritual agreement (Amos 3:3). The goal of our prayer life is spiritual unity, emotional oneness and marital harmony."

"Sharing our spiritual lives," said Joel and Maria Shuler, "is one of the ways we work at being truly intimate. We believe that God wants us to be one, to be united in every way possible. Our total couple intimacy is enhanced by our couple prayer. When we listen in to each other's private conversation with God, we are at our most vulnerable. It is a gift we give to each other, a special time." This is from a couple who found praying together "awkward" at first.

Joel and Maria are Catholics and have been committed to prayer together since Joe's conversion from Judaism some ten years ago. "At first," they recall, "we had to pray mostly traditional prayers" from a book, but Maria knew them so well she would run ahead of Joel. At one point their inability to pray at the same pace struck them as very funny. "We laughed so hard we couldn't continue with the prayer, but the experience freed us up to be more comfortable and natural before the Lord," Maria says.

"We believe that God wants us to be united in mind, heart and body. We work toward unity in every area of our lives, and have much to glean when we share our faith and spirituality with each other. We see how we complement and learn from each other, and thank God for bringing us together. God, Joel and I are like a three-ply cord that is woven and intertwined."[15]

RESOURCES FOR SPIRITUAL INTIMACY

If you're looking for a practical book to assist you in your prayer life, the best one I've found and used is *Conversation with God* by Lloyd Ogilvie (Harvest House).

There are numerous devotional books for individuals to use for their own personal time, and these can be used by couples as well. The daily reading can be read aloud together, or each one can read it individually and then share what it means to him or her. When something you read doesn't connect with you, it's both honest and healthy to say, "Today's devotion just didn't speak to me. Perhaps another time it would." Sometimes my wife, Joyce, and I will comment on what we each read in our own devotional material. Or it could be a passage of Scripture.

Until recently there wasn't very much available in devotional materials for couples. In 1990 the book *Quiet Times for Couples* (Harvest House) was released, and the response to it showed the hunger of couples for something that would help them grow closer spiritually. By reading the daily information aloud to each other, hundreds of thousands of couples have discovered a structure that works for them as well as one that is not overly time-consuming. The material often includes one or two discussion questions to assist couples in applying the Scripture to their marriages.

Reading aloud together as a couple develops an interesting dynamic in the relationship. When you read aloud to each other, you are each aware of what the other has read or heard and you feel a greater sense of motivation to follow what was shared. Reading the Scripture aloud and letting it speak to and guide you in your life will also tend to draw you closer together.

A simple way to implant God's Word in your heart and mind is to take one chapter from a book of the Bible and read it out aloud every day for one month. Why? A speaker I heard in Westmont Chapel in 1958 challenged us by saying, "If you will read the same chapter from the Bible out loud for a month it will be yours for life." He was right. It works. It's one way of following the admonition in Psalm 119:9,11 (*AMP*): "How shall a young man cleanse his way? By taking heed and keeping watch [on himself] according to

Your word [conforming his life to it]. Your word have I laid up in my heart, that I might not sin against You."
Dwight Small summed it up well:

> The lordship of Christ becomes very real when it is known through the Scriptures. Marriage goals are then conformed to the pattern set forth in the believer's relation to Christ. Of all that two people might study and share, nothing can match the influence of God's Word upon their lives.[16]

One of my favorite authors is Max Lucado, particularly because of his penetrating, insightful writing style and his focus on the life and ministry of Jesus. Some of his books include *God Came Near* (Multnomah Books), *No Wonder They Call Him the Savior* (Multnomah Books), *When God Whispers Your Name* (Word Inc.), *The Applause of Heaven* (Word Inc.), and *And the Angels Were Silent* (Walker and Company).

The books *Intimate Moments With the Savior* (NavPress) and *Incredible Moments with the Savior* (NavPress) by Ken Gire are very informative and inspirational. *The Pleasures of God* by John Piper (Multnomah Books) will broaden your own understanding of God, as will *The Knowledge of the Holy* by A. W. Tozer (HarperSanFrancisco).

The following are daily devotional books that can be used by couples in their daily devotions: *100 Portraits of Christ* by Henry Gariepy (Victor Books), *My Daily Appointment With God* by Lucille Fern Sollenberger (Word Inc.), *Hymns for Personal Devotions* by Jerry B. Jenkins (Moody Press), *Quiet Times* by Max F. Anders (Wolgemuth & Hyatt), *God's Best For My Life* by Lloyd Ogilvie (Harvest House), *Two-Part Harmony—A Devotional for Couples* by Patrick M. Morley (Thomas Nelson), and *Quiet Times for Couples* by this author (Harvest House).

NOTES

1. Donald R. Harvey, *The Spiritually Intimate Marriage* (Grand Rapids: Fleming H. Revell, 1991), p. 24.
2. Ibid., pp. 42–45, adapted.
3. Ibid., pp. 45–46.
4. Howard and Jeanne Hendricks, general editors, with LaVonne Neff, *Husbands and Wives*, (Wheaton, Ill.: Victor Books, 1988), p. 158.
5. Harvey, *The Spiritually Intimate Marriage*, pp. 54–56, adapted.

6. Dwight Small, *After You've Said I Do* (Grand Rapids: Fleming H. Revell, 1968), pp. 243–244.

7. Paul Tournier, *The Healing of Persons* (New York: HarperCollins, 1965), pp. 88–89.

8. Small, *After You've Said I Do*, p. 244.

9. Louis H. Evans, *Your Marriage—Duel or Duet?* (Grand Rapids: Fleming H. Revell, 1972), pp. 98–99.

10. From "How to Start and Keep It Going," by Charlie and Martha Shedd, cited by Fritz Ridenour in "Praying Together," *The Marriage Collection* (Grand Rapids: Zondervan Publishers, 1989), pp. 442–443.

11. Carey Moore and Pamela Roswell Moore, *If Two Shall Agree* (Grand Rapids: Chosen Books, Baker Book House, 1992), p. 111.

12. James C. Dobson, *Love for a Lifetime* (Portland, Oreg.: Multnomah Books, 1987), pp. 51–52.

13. Lee Roberts, *Praying God's Will for My Marriage* (Nashville: Thomas Nelson Publishers, 1994), pp. 1, 9, 19, 28, 115, 162, 227, 267.

14. Harry Hollis Jr., *Thank God for Sex* (Nashville: Broadman Press, 1975), pp. 109–111.

15. Moore and Roswell Moore, *If Two Shall Agree*, pp. 194–195.

16. Small, *After You've Said I Do*, p. 243.

How'd They Do That?

We hear so much about couples whose marriages don't last. Often the question is asked, "What went wrong?" Perhaps we've been asking the wrong question. I'd rather know about couples who have *stayed* married, and ask another question: "What did you do right?"

For this reason I decided to look for couples who have been married for a lifetime, and try to discover what they did that made it work. And find them I did. They're all around us. You would be amazed at how many there are. At the church my wife and I attend, there is a Homebuilders class that was started fifty-six years ago. Out of that class alone, fifty-two couples have celebrated their Golden Wedding Anniversaries.

Voices of Experience

For the purpose of this study, I actually ended up interviewing a number of couples from another congregation in Orange County, California, who had been married from forty-seven to sixty-five years. They were asked the following questions:

1. What has been the most fulfilling or positive experience in your marriage? Describe in detail.

2. Describe how you developed your spiritual relationship together.

3. What three things have you done yourself that have helped your marriage?

4. What three things has your spouse done that have helped your marriage?

5. What were (or are) the three greatest adjustments you had to make in marriage and how did you do it?

6. If you could start your marriage over again, what would you do differently?

It was fascinating to hear their stories and see the diversity, yet discover the common themes in these marriages. Even though the couples interviewed began their marriages during much different times, they still have a message to share with the present generation. Most of them married during the Great Depression or during World War II years. They began their marriages during a survival time in our society. The pressures were different, yet similar in many respects.

Listen to some of the selections from their stories. Some were brief, whereas others went into detail. I have let their statements stand largely as they were originally written, feeling that they communicate more realistically than they would with a lot of polishing and editing.

What do you identify with? How is your experience similar or dissimilar? What can you learn from them? And by the way: What will you be able to pass on to the next generation?

Both Trust and Space

One couple married forty-seven years told about the most fulfilling or positive experience in their marriage. They said it was...

"The love we share. I don't think anything surpasses that. I think the biggest thing in our marriage is love and trust, and trust is of utmost importance.

"Our generation is so different from the present one, as in yours everything has to have an answer. I don't think that really falls in at all in our way of thinking and doing. I love her and trust her. You just need to go along and trust each other and love each other every day.

"I think the biggest thing is not to let little things bother you."

Another couple married fifty-four years shared what they did to help their marriage. They said,

"We've allowed each other space, feelings, and ideas that we would discuss and just give each other understanding, supporting one another in ideas and whatever we wanted to do apart. Freedom to be ourselves.

"And communication, I think, is one of the main things. We worked together. Whenever there was a problem, we'd discuss it.

"Having a commitment and the Lord in our lives got us through. We never entertained anything other than this was a lifelong togetherness. And that we would work together and share and support one another. So we didn't consider that an adjustment; it just came natural."

Through Tough Times

A couple married for sixty-five years shared their story.

"We married during the depression in 1929, and those were really tough times. We didn't have one nickel to rub against the other. There just was no money. We couldn't get a job. It was hard on both of us, but we managed.

"I was only out of work for eleven months. We picked up a little extra money on the side by going down to my uncle's farm and bringing chickens back, dressing 'em and selling 'em just to pay bills. That was the Great Depression.

"The Lord just kept us going day by day. Then we had to move in with my wife's mother. I don't know how she put up with us. There were three daughters in a five-room bungalow with an attic, a basement, and one bathroom. And each one had kids.

"But everybody was loving."

The husband shared about his spiritual journey:

"My mother and dad had just started life together on a small farm with one of my sisters who was just a year and a half old. My dad was killed in an accident. I was born two months later and Mother died right after that. I was raised by a great-aunt and great-uncle. But I was church-housed from day one, from what I can recall. I went through what they call catechism and examination, and automatically became a church member.

"When I was about twenty years old, I moved to the Chicago area and I met my wife there. The fellow I was working for, his brother was getting married. He married a girlfriend of hers. That's where we met. Then I started going over to her house, naturally. I went over there one Sunday and she said, 'Are you going to church with us tonight?'

"I said, 'Sure.' They were going to a Baptist church around the corner from her. That's the first time in all those years I heard I had to accept Christ as my Savior. Listening to that preaching all those years and never been told that I had to accept Christ. But from there on I met the Lord, learned to love the Lord, and I've tried to work with Him ever since. Maybe not doing the best that I should, but I've tried.

"I still don't recall us arguing all those years, my wife's mom and dad or any of us.

"Oh, sometimes you'd get angry, you know; it's only natural. But it cools off real fast. You want to kill each other sometimes, but it worked out just fine. We never had any overnight arguments that lasted very long. But we enjoyed each other."

His wife shared that what she did to help the marriage was to have their kids and help raise her husband's nieces and nephews.

"Living a Christian life was the most important part of it. That's what we had to do, because we had a real hard life after we moved to the country. His folks moved in with us. His sister had six months to live and had four children. She moved in with us, and we had the kids for two or three years, four children after she died. The father wouldn't support them. We also had his old aunt who raised him, and she was ninety when she died. And an uncle who was a drunk! Fortunately we didn't have all of these people at the same time.

"Life was hard for many years with all the children, but we still kept trusting the Lord. My old uncle came back to the Lord, too.

"Something else that helped our marriage was we were very good at working together. We always worked together. I always let him think he was the boss and it worked out real good.

"One thing he wouldn't let me do was let me buy anything on time. And I helped him that way. I knew what I would get if I bought anything on time. One thing I hated was for him to scold me.

"And regardless of what we made, when we came to the Lord we felt we should tithe. Even when we only had a dime, we tithed. And I think through that the Lord has helped us, too."

Divorce Wasn't an Option
Another couple explains:

"We've been married forty-seven years. Our most positive experience has been that we have had a mutual love, devotion, and commitment to each other, and to Jesus Christ, as well as for our four children and nine grandchildren.

"There has never been any doubt about our true love for each other and for God. We have each been confident of our faithfulness to one another, without concern or jealousy, and divorce has never been accepted as an option to escape our difficulties.

"Our spiritual progress during our marriage has been staggered. However, it did not present a problem until thirty years ago when one of us knew we had come into a much deeper relationship with Christ, leaving the other mate feeling seriously neglected for some time. When that mate realized through agony, and prayer, that self-control needed to be exercised, and that the other mate was not at the same spiritual high at that same time, and was in fact being neglected, we worked through it with God's help in revealing the truth to us.

"The three things we have done that have helped our marriage have been being completely devoted to my husband, eagerly and joyfully assuming the responsibilities of a homemaker, and I have always tried to keep myself attractive at all times so my husband would be proud of me."

"For me, [the husband] I have never given her cause to worry about my whereabouts, or my association with the opposite sex. I worked diligently to be a good provider, but not at the expense of neglecting time with my family. I've also continually expressed my devotion and loyalty to my wife, our children, and our parents, as being second only to my Lord and God. My career and church responsibilities followed after them, but I have [since my conversion two years after we were married] been a faithful spiritual leader in our home.

"Our greatest adjustments were [in the area of] financial responsibility. In the earlier years of our marriage we did not always agree upon major expenditures and investments. However, over the years confidence was established that the husband had the responsibility, and most of the time profit was realized.

"As a husband, my temper created considerable discord. However, with prayer and discussion, over the years, considerable improvement has been acquired. It has been very important for us to verbally discuss the hurt and embarrassment this problem has created."

"As a wife, my lack of showing affection through touching and caressing, and lack of sexual desire have generated many hurt feelings in the middle and later years of our marriage. Through many agonizing discussions and prayer we have struggled with this problem. God has helped us through prayer to be willing to understand each other, and be willing to die to self. Without our Lord's intervention and support, we may have not have been able to get through those times.

"If we were starting our marriage over again now, as a wife I would not attempt to keep our home in such immaculate condition as to neglect my family's wifely and motherly needs. I would put Christ first, and spend more time with my children and husband. I also would surrender my all to the Lord at the beginning of our marriage, and pay much more attention to my husband, trying more diligently to fulfill his cravings and desires."

"As a husband, I would exercise more self-control in openly expressing my temper, spend even more time with my children in helping them at school, and teaching them the essentials of leading a holy and God-fearing life. I would try to be more sensitive to my wife's fears of my spending too much money on cars and boats. I failed to clarify to her satisfaction that such transactions had hobby benefits to me, as well as being secure and profitable investments."

Commitment Conquered Casualties

A couple married for fifty-eight years shared:

"I think the most fulfilling thing in my life [the husband's] is the fact that my wife has always been committed to me and to our marriage. We haven't really had a lot of bad experiences in our life. We've had a few casualties, but not anything personal or real sad things except loss of family or that kind of thing. But her commitment to our marriage has really been the most fulfilling thing in my life.

"Our spiritual relationship developed by devotions and attending church and being active in church. We always read in the morning from a devotion book, *Bread of Life*, and we have our prayer.

"We have always been involved in church over the years, as a matter of fact, over our whole life, even before we were married. We pray together and if we ever have a problem, we are right there together. I think that's the key to it, to look to each other. When we got married, you got married and were committed to that. That's the way it was going to be.

"The three things that have helped our marriage were our devotion to each other, we always tried to live within our means, and we tried to be a good mom and dad and not cause too much friction.

"When we were married, people didn't have much. If we came from good families, then we had good families. But we didn't have anything, really. And we didn't expect a lot. The Lord has always been good to us. We have had a real successful life, I think. We were committed to each other to start with and we served the Lord at a church doing different things with young people. But the commitment to serving other people, not just ourselves, was important.

"The greatest adjustment we had to make was first living on our income. You wouldn't believe this today, but I was making $2.50 a week when we first got married. We didn't have any debt, and we saved money on that. It's hard to believe, but that's true. We didn't finish up that way, but we started that way.

"[Second,] we had to adjust, basically, to being committed to the other person. We both did the same thing. That was the first adjustment. You're not free anymore. You're committed to a marriage and to loving each other. So it's a different style within our culture. We don't have that today.

"I had to make the adjustment to being responsible for somebody else, too.

"We never really had a serious problem. I know that sounds unbelievable, but it's true. I'm satisfied. I don't think I would do anything differently if we were able to go back. That's not to say that we're perfect, 'cause we're not. But we're human beings that God deals with, and He's brought us along all these years. We've been married for a long, long time. And I hope we have many more years.

"If we had any advice to give to couples, it would be just be true to each other. Love each other. I remember one thing I told my wife, 'If I did anything wrong, and you want to correct me, don't tell anybody else. Tell me first.' And I think she's always done that. Again, we're not perfect. I'm not trying to play it up.

"I think I would tell young couples today that the first thing to do is to make sure you love each other and that the Lord has brought you together to be one. It's easy to make a commitment today and then break it. But if you make a commitment, it's a commitment."

Joint Commitment to Christ
A couple who had been married fifty-two years shared:

"The thing that's meant the most to us from the start is, we knew the Lord. We knew where we were in the Lord as far as who we were responsible to. And when we joined as one, our priority was to serve the Lord Jesus Christ. So regardless of what situation we find ourselves in or have found ourselves in, it's always been a priority in everything. Every decision is made on the basis of how we can best glorify the Lord Jesus Christ—whether it be moves, of which we made many, or whether it be decisions of a family nature.

"We've had joys and we've had sorrows along the way. Our background was such that I felt like we were conditioned for marriage. We were conditioned for those problems that do come up in our lives: the joys, the sorrows, and the changes that have to take place. And I would say the entire span of our marriage has been something that we are very thankful for. We couldn't ask, I don't think, for anything better.

"The thing about it, is the fact that we had not known each other for too long [when we married]. And it was all during the early war years. There were a lot of decisions that had to be made. Whether you get married before you leave, or you wait. And so I'm confident that we made the right decision. We felt that the Lord led us in that. I was gone for the first four years of our marriage, primarily. Before I went overseas, she was able to be with me two or three different times, and so I feel like the Lord led in all of this."

Christ Conquers Physical Problems

A couple married fifty-five years shared:

"I think as we look back over our marriage, one of the most fulfilling things has been the enjoyment of each other. And the fact that God led us together and the fact that even to this day we still enjoy being together.

"Then, our trust in each other. I knew he was faithful—just as much as I knew that I was. And then one of the greatest things of course has been our family—our three boys, even through the trials and tribulations of adolescence.

"And we've just always had that pride in each other's accomplishments, whatever we did.

"Our spiritual relationship started before we were married. I was not a Christian and she was. I did find the Lord. And it's been [something] we've been able to hold onto all of our lives. As a matter of fact, I made that decision before we were married, and she agreed with it, that we would make our friends within the church rather than to cultivate my friends' friendship.

"One thing that hindered us was she had an auto accident five weeks after we were married. She was in a body cast for the first year of our marriage. Her spine had been crushed. We were afraid that had we been kids (we were older, I was twenty-six and she was twenty-three) we would not have stayed together, because that was a difficult time. We borrowed everything we could possibly borrow from the bank. We had no money, but we had each other.

"We always have been able to pray together out loud and really, really know what the other was placing before the Lord. I think our spiritual relationship was developed by putting Christ first. He has been the glue that has really held our marriage together through the physical difficulties."

When asked about what they had done to help their marriage, the wife shared:

"It took many years financially to come out of the accident. And I was willing to go back to teaching. Well, I loved it! But I was willing to go back to teach even though we had a family. I think that was a help in our marriage. And I know that I tried to live within our means. I know that I really tried to make a happy home and not [have] a long list of things when he came home to jump on him, whether it be what the kids had done or what happened. It was more of the positive things we shared. Of course we shared the negative, too. We have a plaque that says 'Happiness is homemade.' And that is so true. But unhappiness is also homemade."

The husband shared:

"Well, I guess my work habits had a lot to do with it. I worked long hours, but when I came home, as she said, she had a pleasant place for me to be. She had food ready at the table. And we took lots of trips. We had a happy family. We had some family troubles, maybe. But I think that would be my main thing. We have always kept Christ [at the] center in our family, too."

His wife added:

"The things that I felt that he put into our marriage were his great patience and his unselfishness of putting his family first to his best ability. You always knew what he was going to be like. He wasn't up in the clouds and then down. I could always depend on him being the same. When he came home from work, I didn't have to worry or bite my nails thinking, *What's going to happen today that's going to make him tired?* or anything like that.

"Then his patience with me was wonderful. I was in a brace for about six years off and on, and he had great patience with me and understanding. When I would have to lie down and take it easy for awhile, he never looked at me or came through the room saying, 'Are you down again?' or 'Here you go again' or anything like that.

"Then he had the first of a series of heart attacks before heart surgery when he was just in his early forties. I think our physical difficulties gave us both an understanding. We were both given enough physical limitations, handicaps you may say, even though we've never felt that the other one was handicapped even with his stroke."

They talked about their greatest adjustments. The husband said,

"I think my greatest adjustment for the first six weeks was going from the single life to the married life. I had always been in a home where I did what I wanted, when I wanted, how I wanted. My folks seemed to depend on me for that. And then, being married at twenty-six, I had made my own decisions. I never consulted anyone else. It was hard for me to consider anyone else after

I got married, because I could do and come and go. I would always come home, but it was hard for me to let her in on what I was doing, financially or whatever.

"After the [accident], our first year was dictated for us. We had no money; she lost her job. I didn't have enough money. I had a good job, but it wasn't enough to pay the doctor bills. So that was a tough adjustment. It was kind of a forced adjustment. We just did it."

The wife shared,

"I think that was the hardest thing for me, too. If we had just been out of high school, just kids, our marriage probably wouldn't have lasted with my being down and having to be hospitalized for a long time. Then having to go back to living with my parents was an adjustment. When we look back, we are so thankful that it didn't happen when we had our children or later in life.

"And I think, of course, about his stroke, although we're so thankful it isn't worse, we're so thankful his mind wasn't affected. That has been an adjustment. The retirement hasn't been an adjustment for us, because he's never really retired. So this adjusting to his stroke at this time of life has been one of the hardest. But then it's just day by day. We have each other. We look at so many of our friends who have lost their mates. We've just been so thankful. It has been hard for him. Because you grieve with any loss. And acceptance comes after that grief."

Her husband shared,

"I have to fight pity parties. I don't have many, but I do fight having them. When you get an arm that won't work and a leg that won't work, and to begin with, my side wasn't working, and I couldn't talk, you go through quite a bit."

"I Would Have Made More Cornbread"

The husband continued:

"If I were starting my marriage over, I couldn't really think of anything I would do differently. I was in love with her when I married her and I have been every minute since then. But I think I would try communicating [better], sharing what I was doing better. That would be the one thing I would do.

"Also, rather than making a decision, I would talk it over with her before I make it. I think [those are] the only things I would change."

In concluding this interview, his wife said,

"And I think our earlier years and up 'til the recent years in our disagreements, I had the very ugly habit of bringing up past things. Not just disagreeing on what we were disagreeing about, but bringing up, 'Well, if you hadn't done that' or 'If I hadn't done that' or 'If we hadn't done that, such and such wouldn't have been' and all of that. But I did not hold grudges. I truly learned to overcome that. I think I would say sooner, 'I'm sorry.'

"I knew he loved little white navy beans and ham and cornbread. So I knew that when we needed to make up, I needed to make navy beans and ham and cornbread. And I think I would just make more cornbread."

"WE WILL MAKE IT WORK"

These couples have probably seen and experienced more change in their life-times as couples than any previous generation. It wasn't easy for them. But something held them together. Perhaps the theme that runs through these few examples and the hundreds of other stories I've heard over the years is that concept emphasized earlier in the book—commitment. For these couples, divorce was not an option. Instead, there was an attitude of "We will make it work."

I've often wondered what it would be like if we lived in a society that did not have anything called divorce. What if it just didn't exist? You were totally and fully bound and committed for life, till death do you part. But then I realized, we do! As Christians, our perspective of the world is different from that of nonbelievers. Scripture tells us, "Do not be conformed to this world" (Rom. 12:2, *NKJV*). We are called to be different. And that difference means building a marriage that lasts, regardless.

Incompatible couples don't have to divorce, for all couples are incompatible to some degree.

An affair doesn't have to destroy a marriage. Yes, it may be painful and violate trust, but it also provides the opportunity for a couple to experience repentance, God's grace, forgiveness, and restoration. I have seen dozens of couples who have recovered from unfaithfulness, and today have strong marriages that reflect the presence of Jesus Christ.

Abusive marriages don't have to result in divorce when there is repentance.

Some couples look for reasons to justify the dissolution of their marriages. I've had couples tell me their marriages are painful because it's chaotic. My response? Let God do what He did in the creation of the world. "In the beginning, God created out of chaos...." And He still does.

I've had couples tell me that dissolving their marriage was necessary to take away the pain and allow them to experience joy. Recently, though, I came across an illustration written by a friend. In all four Gospels there is the story of the rich young ruler who came to Jesus and asked Him what he must do to inherit eternal life. Jesus told him what he must do, but he was not willing to do what Jesus said. The Gospel writers saw what happened, for Mark 10:22 says, "At this the man's face fell. He went away sad, because he had great wealth" *(NIV)*.

But in another portion of Scripture (see Luke 19), we read the account of another rich man, Zacchaeus. He accepted Jesus' invitation, repented, and did what Jesus asked.

Describing the differences in these two events, my friend wrote:

> One man left in sorrow and the other embraced Jesus with joy. What do these two passages illustrate? Simply this: There is no joy in moving apart—*there is only joy in coming together.*
>
> No one walks away—whether it be from spiritual light, a relationship with God, or a marriage—with happiness. Walking away is always accompanied by sorrow and oftentimes regret. There is no joy found in moving apart. Joy is only found in coming together—in accepting spiritual light, in embracing the arms of the Savior, and in restoring strained relationships. There is joy—true joy—in reconciliation.
>
> Reconciliation is God's grand spiritual design. It is a focal point in Scripture throughout both Old and New Testaments. It is why Jesus came—to provide a way whereby man could be reconciled to God. It is God's plan and goal. It should be our way of life; we are to live reconciled lives. When there is reconciliation, whether it be between God and man or within a marriage, there is joy—true joy.[1]

What about you? What can you do to move closer to Jesus Christ? To your spouse?

Incidentally—what do you want to be able to say about your marriage when you've been married as long as the couples who shared in this chapter? Give it some thought. Now is the time to be doing what needs to be done so you can say, "It was very worthwhile." Perhaps the following poem sums up what the couples in this chapter have been saying and will give you an idea of what can be said after you've been married fifty years.

On the Eve of Their Golden Wedding Day
John C. Bonser

"Our Golden Wedding Day draws near,"
   the husband said.
The elderly woman, smiling, raised her head,
"Will you write me a poem as you used to do?
That's the gift I'd like most from you!"

The old man, agreeing, limped from the room,
Went out on the porch in the twilight's gloom,

Leaned on the railing and reminisced:
"Often we sat here, shared hopes, and kissed.

"Dear Lord, how the years have hurried by—
Those memories of youth make an old man sigh!
Now we grow weary and bent and gray,
What clever words can I possibly say

"To show that I love her just as much
As I did when her cheeks were soft to my touch,
When her eyes were bright and her lips were warm,
And we happily walked with her hand on my arm!"

So the husband stood while the evening breeze
Echoed his sigh through the nearby trees
Till the joys they had shared in days long past
Merged into thoughts he could voice at last,

And he went inside and got paper and pen;
Sat down at the kitchen table and then
Carefully wrote what his wife had desired:
A gift as "golden" as a love inspired.

    "Sweetheart, dear wife, my closest friend,
    With you my days begin and end.
    Though time has stolen strength and youth,
    It cannot change this shining truth:
    Our love has lasted all these years
    While hardships came and sorrow's tears.
    We've met each test and gotten by,
    And I will love you till I die!
    We are not rich in worldly wealth
    But we own nothing gained by stealth,
    And you remain my greatest treasure,
    My source of pride and quiet pleasure.
    I wish you all the happiness
    With which two loving hearts are blessed;
    You were, and are, my choice for life,
    My girl, my lady, my sweet wife!"

The poem finished, the husband arose,
Went into the room where his good wife dozed

And tenderly kissing her nodding head,
"Wake up, 'sleeping beauty,' and come to bed!"[2]

NOTES

1. Donald Harvey, Surviving Betrayal (Grand Rapids: Baker Books, 1995), pp. 36–37.
2. Used by permission of the author, John C. Bonser, of Florissant, Missouri.

APPENDIX

Instructions

Answer each of these eleven questions. Then fill in the Satisfaction Scale that follows. After both of you have completed these two exercises, select a time when you can be together privately and share your responses. Covering each item may require two or three sessions. Be sure to focus on what you want and what you can do for the future.

1. Describe how much significant time you spend together as a couple, and when you spend it.
2. Describe five behaviors or tasks your partner does that you appreciate.
3. List five personal qualities of your spouse that you appreciate.
4. How frequently do you affirm or reinforce your spouse for the behaviors and qualities described in numbers two and three?
5. List four important requests you have for your spouse at this time. How frequently do you make these requests? What is your spouse's response?
6. List four important requests your spouse has for you at this time. How frequently does he/she make these requests? What is your response?
7. What do you appreciate most about your partner's communication?
8. What do you do to let your spouse know that you love him/her?
9. What does your spouse do to let you know he/she loves you?
10. What has been one of the most fulfilling experiences in your marriage?
11. What personal and marital behaviors would you like to change in yourself?

SATISFACTION SCALE

Instructions

Use an X to indicate your level of satisfaction in each element of your relationship listed below, with O = no satisfaction, 5 = average, and 10 = super, fantastic, the best.

Use a circle to indicate what you think your partner's level of satisfaction is at the present time.

1. Our daily personal involvement with each other.

o   1   2   3   4   5   6   7   8   9   10

2. Our affectionate romantic interaction.

o   1   2   3   4   5   6   7   8   9   10

3. Our sexual relationship.

o   1   2   3   4   5   6   7   8   9   10

4. The frequency of our sexual contact.

o   1   2   3   4   5   6   7   8   9   10

5. My trust in my spouse.

o   1   2   3   4   5   6   7   8   9   10

6. My spouse's trust in me.

o   1   2   3   4   5   6   7   8   9   10

7. The depth of our communication together.

o   1   2   3   4   5   6   7   8   9   10

8. How well we speak one another's language.

o   1   2   3   4   5   6   7   8   9   10

9. The way we divide chores.

o   1   2   3   4   5   6   7   8   9   10

10. The way we make decisions.

o   1   2   3   4   5   6   7   8   9   10

11. The way we manage conflict.

o   1   2   3   4   5   6   7   8   9   10

12. Adjustment to one another's differences.

   o   1   2   3   4   5   6   7   8   9   10

13. Amount of free time together.

   o   1   2   3   4   5   6   7   8   9   10

14. Quality of free time together.

   o   1   2   3   4   5   6   7   8   9   10

15. Amount of free time apart.

   o   1   2   3   4   5   6   7   8   9   10

16. Our interaction with friends as a couple.

   o   1   2   3   4   5   6   7   8   9   10

17. The way we support each other in rough times.

   o   1   2   3   4   5   6   7   8   9   10

18. Our spiritual interaction.

   o   1   2   3   4   5   6   7   8   9   10

19. Our church involvement.

   o   1   2   3   4   5   6   7   8   9   10

20. The level of our financial security.

   o   1   2   3   4   5   6   7   8   9   10

21. How we manage money.

   o   1   2   3   4   5   6   7   8   9   10

22. My spouse's relationship with my relatives.

   o   1   2   3   4   5   6   7   8   9   10

23. My relationship with my spouse's relatives.

   o   1   2   3   4   5   6   7   8   9   10

Select any three responses that have a score of 3 or less, and indicate what needs to occur for you to have a higher level of satisfaction. Also discuss how you have tried to work on this issue.

Marriage and Family Building Resources from H. Norman Wright

Communication: Key to Your Marriage

By H. Norman Wright

Couples will immediately begin to improve their communication skills as they follow Norm Wright's steps toward resolving marital conflicts and growing in togetherness.

Paperback • ISBN 08307.17137
Group Study Guide • ISBN 08307.17129

The Power of a Parent's Words

By H. Norman Wright

Teaches parents ways to meet a child's unique needs with words of life and hope.

Hardcover • ISBN 08307.14340

Mothers, Sons and Wives

By H. Norman Wright

Learn to understand the mother-son relationship and the impact it has on husbands and wives.

Paperback • ISBN 08307.18060

Holding on to Romance

By H. Norman Wright

Every married person wants to hold on to romance. But often romance can slip away. Here's how that special and elusive feeling can be recaptured.

Paperback • ISBN 08307.15770

Questions Women Ask in Private

By H. Norman Wright

In **Questions Women Ask in Private**, Norm Wright gives you clear, concise answers to more than 100 questions Christian counselors are hearing from women across the country.

Trade • ISBN 08307.16378

Always Daddy's Girl

By H. Norman Wright

Every woman wonders how her father affected her.

"We highly recommend **Always Daddy's Girl**."—Gary Smalley and John Trent, Ph.D.

Trade • ISBN 08307.13549

The Marriage Renewal Video Series

From H. Norman Wright

For couples who want to expand their communication skills, rekindle the fires of romance or learn their mates' language. These dynamic video seminars can help couples individually or in groups.

Communication: Key to Your Marriage
Video
SPCN 85116.00787

Holding on to Romance
Video
SPCN 85116.00779

How to Speak Your Spouse's Language
Video
SPCN 85116.00795

Ask for these resources at your local Christian bookstore.